MW00442058

LEGENDARY
DEER CAMPS

"Hunter's Fire"
by Ken Laager

ROBERT WEGNER

© 2001 by Robert Wegner

All rights reserved. No portion of this publication may be reproduced or
transmitted in any form or by any means, electronic or mechanical, including
photocopying, recording, or any information storage and retrieval system
without permission in writing from the publisher, except by a reviewer who
may quote brief passages in a critical article or review to be printed in a
magazine or newspaper, or electronically transmitted on radio or television.

Published by

krause
publications
700 East State Street • Iola, WI 54990-0001
715/445-2214 • FAX: 715/445-4087 www.krause.com

Please call or write for a free catalog of publications. The toll-free number to
place an order or to request a free catalog is (800) 258-0929, or use our regular
business number (715) 445-2214.
Library of Congress Catalog Number: 2001091059
ISBN: 0-87341-992-8
Printed in Canada

For Maren Wegner — my best deer hunting partner and gourmet chef of venison cuisine at Deer Valley.

Rob Wegner Photo Collection.

CONTENTS

Awhile back a sadistic sociologist presented Maryland hunters a tough choice. On a survey he asked if they would rather hunt with their buddies where there were few deer or hunt alone where there were many more deer. After pondering this question, more than two-thirds of the hunters said they would rather hunt with their buddies.

That single statistic says something basic about modern deer hunting, and it tells me a lot about why my family continues to hunt along the Conley road.

Heberleins started hunting in Ashland County when the only deer in Wisconsin lived in the Northern Forest. Uncle Carl and his buddy Jerry would go up by train. They stayed at the Cayuga Hotel until 1948 when they bought an abandoned farm on the Conley road. I can remember the early '50s and my dad's snow-covered blue Ford pickup truck returning from the North full of Christmas trees to sell at his gas station. More often than not, some dead deer were tucked among those trees. Not only did deer live along the Conley road, there were a lot of them. The cutover, the slash and the fires that followed made excellent whitetail habitat, and you could

"We know there are better places to hunt deer, but we hunt them here because this is where my dad built our cabin." Professor Tom Heberlein, right, with campmate Lyman Wible at Old Tamarack Lodge on the Conley road in northwestern Wisconsin, November 1999.

easily see deer. Most camps planned to shoot a doe, usually before the season, for "camp meat." And they did.

Over the years, the forest grew back deep and thick. Deer spread all over the state, becoming a pest animal in cities and in farm country. Meanwhile, along the Conley road, the deer density plummeted to fewer than five per square mile — and you could no longer see them. Men brought stews cooked by their wives. Johnnie Kerr, the grocer who hunted with us, horded and aged big steaks the month before the season. In some years, our logbook had more pictures of steaks than deer. Many seasons the whole camp was skunked. I recently went 14 straight days without seeing a deer. Around the fire at night, we tell "red squirrel stories" — long tales where the heart-stopping "crunch, crunch, crunch" in the brush turns out to be nothing more than a red squirrel.

Why do the Heberleins, the Matuszaks, the Graunkes and the Hansons come back and hunt the Conley road year after year? Why aren't they rational predators following the abundance? The Maryland data tell the story. Most hunters choose friends over deer. The deer are nice. They need to be there. Occasionally, a big one, like Ben's Buck, hangs on the rack. The camp is where old men tell stories, and boys grow to be men. That is where you hunt deer. Not where whitetails run around like bunny rabbits. Deer camps are timeless. Lyman sat back one night in our camp and said "Jeeze, this could be 1975 or 1955." Once a year we set the clock back 20 years or so, to a simpler time. It is called "Deer Camp."

The Wisconsin deer hunt is about deer camp. One survey I did showed that more than half of the deer hunters in Wisconsin hunt from a camp. The "camp" could be a drafty motel room in Park Falls where my friend Jim and his son hunted; or the Heinze farm in Lewiston Township, where the extended family congregates yearly to kill and butcher a score or more of deer. Even though the deer have come to the cities, the Wisconsin hunters leave their homes for "Camp."

So, why are there so many books about deer and so few books about hunting camps? It is partly because deer hunters aren't nearly as pretty as deer. Deer are nice to look at, but scruffy hunters in blaze-orange clown suits are not the stuff for coffee tables. Deer hunting techniques have greatly improved as hunters eagerly read how-to books, but the application of science and technology to the art of deer hunting has not yet taught us how to create a suitable camp.

It seems to me that a good deer camp needs multiple generations, with old men to tell the stories and young men to sit and listen with wide eyes. It needs some serious hunters to make the new stories, and some camp men to make sure the floors are swept and the dishes washed. I am not sure of much else. Although I am a sociologist, I hunt deer during the season and have not snooped around many camps in the name of science. This would be a good project for a young anthropologist, I think.

Fortunately, Rob Wegner is trying to even the score with those deer books, and advance knowledge a bit with these stories of America's legendary camps. Aldo Leopold had a deer camp, and so did Bill Faulkner. Professors and poets take to the forest. But there is more to it than that. Think about your camp. This is the time once a year when a group of men (and now and then, some women) come together to tell stories of the past, and to talk of deer and of snow and the forest. To brag. To share.

Think of the quiet times drying dishes, where advice is sought and given. Recall the long drive north where we catch up on what went on in busy lives during the past year. Deer camps are full of games, old jokes and sometimes pranks.

And then the old men die, and the boy who just last year it seems shot his first deer is the lead hunter, making the plan and walking up on a deer in the thick forest when all else fails. The old cabin is replaced by new, but the camp remains.

Read about the camps of others, but think of your own. It is those memories we are creating with the deer hunt, and those are the ones we take with us.

— *Tom Heberlein*
Kemp Natural Resources Station
Woodruff, Wis.

PALACE IN THE POPPLE

By John Madson

It's a smoky, raunchy boars' nest
With an unswept, drafty floor
And pillowticking curtains
And knife scars on the door.
The smell of pine-knot fire
From a stovepipe that's come loose
Mingles sweetly with the bootgrease
And the Copenhagen snoose.

There are work-worn .30-30s
With battered, steel-shod stocks,
And drying lines of longjohns
And of steaming, pungent socks.
There's a table for the Bloody Four
And their game of two-card draw,
And there's deep and dreamless sleeping
On bunk ticks stuffed with straw.

Jerry and Jake stand by the stove,
Their gun-talk loud and hot,
And Bogie has drawn a pair of kings,
And is raking in the pot.
Frank's been drafted again as cook
And is peeling some spuds for stew
While Bruce wanders by in baggy drawers
Reciting "Dan McGrew."

No where on Earth is fire so warm
Nor coffee so infernal,
Nor whiskers so stiff, jokes so rich,
Nor hope blooming so eternal.
A man can live for a solid week
In the same old underbritches
And walk like a man and spit when he wants
And scratch himself when he itches.

I tell you, boys, there's no place else
Where I'd rather be, come fall,
Where I eat like a bear and sing like a wolf
And feel like I'm bull-pine tall.
In that raunchy cabin out in the bush
In the land of the raven and loon,
With a tracking snow lying new to the ground
At the end of the rutting moon.

ROMANCING THE DEER CAMP

Deer Camp. The very words exude excitement, romance and adventure. The call of "Daylight in the Swamp!" brings back memories of my early deer-camp experiences in northern Wisconsin in the late 1950s, a time when schools closed for deer season and boys saw deer camp as more fun than Christmas.

In his essay "Deercamp" in *God, Guns & Rock 'N' Roll* (2000), Ted Nugent describes deer camp as "rocket fuel for the fires of life."

In *Legendary Deer Camps*, I explore the fires of excitement, allure and ambiance of 11 legendary deer camps whose roots run deep into our past. These sacred places represent the spirit of the American deer camp, whether they're in a Mississippi Delta bayou with William Faulkner or in the Dakota Badlands with Theodore Roosevelt.

Deer hunters will find much in the stories of these camps that could have been written last November, and they will recognize many of the personalities of their own deer hunting buddies. All of the camps are magical places well known for rites, rituals, camaraderie and buck-hunting tales.

In them, we see basic elements of the American deer camp: mist, fog, moonshine, a bending meat-pole, lines of Winchester rifles, and the aromas of venison, onions and wood smoke.

At night, like any stag party, deer hunters in these camps sang, played cards, told lies, drank whiskey, argued about politics, and swapped stories around the campfire. Deer camps became great social equalizers where class barriers were breached for the period of the deer hunt.

The essence of deer camp consists of stories, memories, and endless talk of deer rifles and big phantom bucks. The camps act as a safety valve, a guarantee of sanity allowing grown men to act like little boys while reliving and re-creating deer hunting's cultural past. These camps reflect not only an American institution, but a state of mind. While in camp, hunters share not only an affinity with whitetails, but with other hunters in the context of the rutting moon, tarpaper shacks, wood smoke, starry nights, crackling fires, pot-belly stoves, frying onions, venison liver, boot grease, sweaty socks and whispering pines. Deer camp is indeed "a time of tall imaginings and grand expectations" as Vermont deer hunter John Randolph called it.

Rough camaraderie, old pickups, hand-drawn maps, polished snowshoes, lines of racked deer rifles, and antlers of well-remembered bucks nailed to the wall all enhance the romance. Each of the chapters to follow details these ingredients of the American deer camp — a great cultural institution.

In looking at these deer camps, we must reshape our image of man the deer hunter, and acquire a new perception of who we are. We need to retrieve and honor our deer camp heritage, for it constitutes the essence of who we are as deer hunters. We cannot physically return to history's great deer camps. Instead, we must remember the words of hunter/naturalist Paul Shepard, who reminds us in *Coming Home to the Pleistocene* (1998) that any culture is a mosaic that preserves and reincorporates key features of earlier ways of life.

This book attempts to do just that.

Our current disconnection from our great past undermines deer hunting's acceptability in modern society. Without rites, rituals, significant ceremony and preservation of historical artifacts, recreational deer hunting will continue to decline.

We must also remember that in deer hunting, man ultimately returns to his old homestead, be it a hollow log, a log cabin, a tarpaper shack on the back 40, a canvas wall tent in the balsams, or a lean-to built by early 1800s voyageurs. It is in such sacred places that the hunter restores an alertness he can nowhere else achieve amid the discontentments of today's civilization.

— *Robert Wegner*
Deer Valley, April 1, 2001

THE BUCK HORN TAVERN

"**Poor fellow,** he no doubt was in hopes that when the shades of evening come on ... he might seek refreshment and repose during the night. But the worshiper of the God Bow-waw-nee was on his track, and his fate was sealed. He had coursed for the last time the dark forest of Middleburgh, and his eyes were soon to forever close on his favorite 'stamping grounds.'"

— Oliver Hazard Perry,
Hunting Expeditions of Oliver Hazard Perry. Jan. 28, 1843.

Kenyon C. Bolton III.

With those words of warning directed toward white-tailed bucks, and with his primitive rifle belching staccato reports, Oliver Hazard Perry (1817-1864) of Ohio pursued his region's deer.

This robust, rugged deerslayer from Cleveland called deer "Old Hemlock Rangers," and he hunted them with the vitality and intensity of Richard Wagner's "The Flying Dutchman."

Perry didn't shoot deer. He "put their lights out!" In his deer-hunting diary, posthumously published in 1899 and limited to 100 copies, Perry recounts his annual deer hunts in Michigan and Ohio between 1836 and 1855. His hunts lasted two to three months in the vast, unbroken wilderness forests bordering Lake Erie and Lake Huron. There, he tramped through cedar swamp after cedar swamp, eventually arriving at Simeon Newton's Buck Horn Tavern three miles from Tuscola, Mich., and south of the Cass River. "Buck horns" nailed to the meat pole answered for the tavern's sign. Perry went there to eat venison and potatoes, and drink snake-root whiskey.

Perry described the Buck Horn Tavern as a low, solitary log cabin on an isolated road next to a vast woods 4 miles wide. This pleasant and comfortable backwoods tavern could accommodate six deer hunters. The log building contained two large rooms: a barroom and a kitchen. The sleeping quarters were directly under the roof. Perry referred to its owner, Simeon Newton, as a "portly, fine-looking man and an expert deer hunter." Perry said Mrs. Newton was a fine cook of venison tenderloins.

Perry hunted deer with Simeon Newton and his boys, and hung his deer with pride on the Buck Horn Tavern's meat pole. The Buck Horn became his Shangri-la. When bad weather prohibited deer hunting, he spent countless days in front of its blazing fireplace reading novels and sporting literature. The Buck Horn Tavern, located near Perry's permanent deer camp on the Cass River, served as the social centerpiece for his legendary deer hunting expeditions in

State Historical Society of Wisconsin

Michigan.

Perry's beloved deer shanty on the Cass River, as seen in Dr. Elisha Sterling's illustration, rested on what the state surveyor called "swamp sand," which was valued at 12 cents an acre in the 1850s. Between 1853 and 1860, Perry and Dr. Sterling, a gifted surgeon from Cleveland, chased bucks each year from Indian summer to mid-December for recreation and consumption.

At this old log shanty, buck antlers were nailed to a meat pole as a sign for customers to dine on venison and potatoes and drink snake-root whiskey.

From his Cass River camp, Perry and Dr. Sterling often canoed down to Tuscola to wine and dine, and then canoed back to camp in the moonlight. If not satisfied with their Tuscola supper, they would build a blazing oak fire, cut the tenderloins from a deer, and cook them on a stick before retiring for the evening.

To reach his cherished deer hunting turf, Perry traveled by rail cars, cutters, horses, sleighs, steamboats, stages and canoes. He slept wherever people would keep him, or inside hollow trees lined with straw and large coonskin robes. Most often, though, he stayed at rural taverns, the centerpieces of the deerslayers' tradition, and the focal points of all deer-camp conversation. In his

Claiming the Shot: After the Hunt in the Adirondacks by John George Brown, 1865. A white-tailed deer hunt was a serious, intellectual affair that entailed adventure, romance and a love for natural history. In this painting, the hunters study and admire a downed buck.

journal, Perry named 13 country taverns that provided bed and breakfast for deerslayers. After a stiff drink of "Old Bald Eye" at such places as the Buck Horn or Beebee's Tavern on the South Ridge, Perry played euchre with fellow hunters and talked about "flocks of deer."

After traveling for days with his sorrel mare and cutter, as well as his dogs Hunter and Sport, Perry hunted deer in places such as Bear Swamp, Black Swamp, Podunk Swamp and the great Cottonwood Swamp. After the hunt, he "bent" his way to the backwoods taverns as daylight faded. Many of Perry's hunts ended at such legendary taverns as Corslet's Log Tavern, 20 miles

The Detroit Institute of Art.

from Hillsdale, Mich., on the Indiana Road; Furney's Tavern in Bellevue, Ohio; Kinny's Tavern on French Creek in Avon Centre, Ohio; and Walker's Stone Tavern in Parma, Ohio.

There he finished the day with pie, whiskey, cheese and venison tenderloins on oak coals. He also indulged in the luxury of pipe smoking. Other deer hunts ended in rustic deer shanties made with hemlock boughs covered with innu-merable deer horns.

Because no biographic or contemporary accounts exist on Perry, we know little about his early life. He was born April 12, 1817, the same year Solomon Sweatland — one of Ohio's legendary deerslayers — confronted a massive 10-point buck in the choppy waters of Lake Erie off the shoreline of Ashtabula County.

During his boyhood, Perry listened to stories about a deer-hunting adventure in which deer-slayer Sweatland lost a dramatic deer-man skirmish. Then, with canoe paddle in hand, he endured gale-force winds and cold, and turbulent waters that whipped his 14-foot dugout canoe like a piece of driftwood across Lake Erie to the Canadian shore. There, after a week filled with trauma and misadventure, this pioneer farmer of the Western Reserve boarded the schooner *Fire Fly* for Ashtabula Harbor. He then returned to Sweatland's Clearing in Ohio's northeastern corner, a short distance below the mouth of Conneaut Creek. He was welcomed with a standing ovation and a three-gun salute, possibly because he had missed the preacher's reading of the 21st Psalm and his own funeral oration by two days.

Perry's well-to-do parents christened him with the same name as the famous Commodore Oliver Hazard Perry (1785-1819), the naval hero of the War of 1812. This grand-nephew of Commodore Perry spent his childhood in the wild and rural atmosphere of Cleveland in Ohio's Cuyahoga County.

In December 1818, members of Perry's family and other fellow Clevelanders joined settlers and pioneer deer hunters from neighboring villages for a massive deer drive. It came to be known in the annals of American deer hunting as "The Great Hinckley Deer Hunt." After several weeks of intense meetings and detailed plans, the drive commenced at sunrise on Dec. 24, 1818. That Christmas Eve day dawned crisp and cold with nearly 600 heavily armed men and boys taking part. The entourage was divided into four divisions, which were led by four captains, "one of whom had Supreme Command of the entire battalion," Captain Milton P. Pierce noted in an article in the *American Field*.

Armed with axes, lances, knives, hatchets, horns, hounds, flintlock rifles, Jaeger muskets, and bayonets mounted on poles, the Hinckley deerslayers formed a huge square embracing the Township of Hinckley. The four lines of drivers formed a continuous line for 20 miles and moved everything within its confines toward the township's center. As bugles and deer hounds sounded their cries, deer ran in every direction. The officers cautioned the hunters to fire low and toward the center. Only one hunter, "Big Red" Seymour, was wounded. He received a load of buckshot in his shoulder, but his flesh wound allowed him to continue with the deer drive in an upright position.

When the noisy rattle of musketry ended and the smoke cleared, more than 300 white-tailed deer, 21 bears and 17 wolves lay dead on the forest floor. After a final trumpet call, a quick roll-call was taken by one of Perry's descendants, only 454 hunters answered the call. The rest of the group, 146 drivers, remained in the brush.

The Arkites meet to discuss the classic sporting literature of the day.

Western Reserve Historical Society.

Rob Wegner Photo Collection.

The closing days of the Buck Horn, circa 1870. With the advent of the railroad, backwoods taverns like the Buck Horn began to fall by the wayside.

William Coggswell, of Bath, Ohio — a prince of huntsmen — soon appeared with several men. They brought along a barrel of whiskey, which was drawn in a sled by a yoke of oxen. The men built a rousing fire and the scene "turned into one of boisterous jubilation and merriment," as a historian recalled in the 1883 *History of Medina County*. Word soon circulated that the entourage would camp there for the night. The sweet aroma of roasting venison soon led to song, speeches and amazing anecdotes of deer-hunting adventure and pioneer life. And then, "Riley the Rover" of Cleveland, the great bard of the entire affair, stepped forth and described the scene:

They set the barrel on one end,
And stove the other in;
They used for tapster to attend
A ladle made of tin.
The whiskey, made by honest men,
Was drank by men upright,
And none would deem it hurtful then
To drink on such a night.

Then every man drank what he chose,
And all were men of spunk;
But not a fighting wrangle rose,
And not a man got drunk.

By the time Perry entered his teens in this adventurous atmosphere, his curiosity and interest in wildlife and natural history were well established. He gradually matured into a respected naturalist, solidly versed in the habits and habitats of white-tailed deer in Ohio and Michigan. He found ample opportunity to satisfy his curiosity about whitetails while wandering the banks of the Cuyahoga River and its tributaries, as well as the forest wilderness around his home.

I n 1836, the 19-year-old Perry joined a club of like-minded young men interested in hunting and natural history. They met to share and exchange information on their daily

tramps afield. Club members collected natural-history specimens, and read the great sporting literature of the time, especially William T. Porter's *Spirit of the Times* (1830-1861) and John S. Skinner's *American Turf Register and Sporting Magazine* (1829-1844). These were the first two sportsmen's journals of the period that published great deer hunting epistles.

Such names as John James Audubon, William Elliott and Henry William Herbert (Frank Forester) graced the pages of these journals. Also writing in these magazines were lesser-known deerslayers named Ringwood, Hawk-Eye, Wah-O-Pe-Kah, Tarkill, Acteon, Elderado and Natty Bumppo. In fact, Oliver Hazard Perry himself, writing under the pen name "Old Stout," contributed articles. These stories and letters to the editors were interspersed with the hunting poetry of Sir Walter Scott, Greek and Latin verse, biblical quotations and high-level prose from Shakespeare to Euripides.

Club members eventually called themselves the Arkites, and developed into a prestigious social, cultural and sporting organization that met to discuss sporting literature. They read Audubon's essay "Deer Hunting," which was widely reprinted at the time, as well as William Elliott's *Carolina Sports by Land and Water* (1846). They also enjoyed Frank Forester's sketches that dealt with his deer shooting escapades near the Dutchman's Tavern in the woodlands of Orange County, N.Y.

Perry first hunted whitetails in December 1836. This four-day hunt took place in Avon, 18 miles west of Cleveland near Kinny's Tavern on

A.F. Tait, 1880. *Deer*. Collection of the Shelburne Museum, Shelburne, Vt.

French Creek. There he shot his first buck — a 10-pointer — in the Great Tamarack Swamp. He recorded the incident in his journal and affixed to it a rare woodcut engraving of a white-tailed buck by Dr. Alexander Anderson (1775-1870), a well-known artist and creator of America's first wood engravings. For the next 20 years, Perry painstakingly recorded his everyday activities in the Ohio and Michigan forests, and complemented the text with Anderson's woodcuts. Not content to just record the activities of the chase, Perry enhanced his journal with intimate details of the scenes and people encountered along the way.

Perry's journal likely represents the most colorful descriptions ever penned by an early American deerslayer. Of the more than 1,100 volumes listed on deer and deer hunting in *Wegner's Bibliography on Deer and Deer Hunting, 1413-1992* (1992), the author considers Perry's adventure diary to be his most cherished blue-chip deer book. It is one of the rarest sporting books ever published, and an original edition costs $2,000 or more.

Many out-of-print booksellers remain unaware of its existence. Only 100 copies were printed in 1899, and only a fraction of these can be accounted for. Among the owners are the Library of Congress and the Sheldon Collection at Yale. In addition, the University of Michigan and the Western Reserve Historical Society in Cleveland also have original copies.

Perry's diaries have remained hidden for almost a century. Thanks to the untiring efforts

State Historical Society of Wisconsin.

Country taverns served as a social centerpiece of the early American deer hunting experience till the end of the 19th century.

of publisher John Howard, a reprinted edition was published by St. Hubert's Press in 1994.

Perry's deer-hunting narratives are a valuable addition to American deer-hunting literature from 1836 to 1855. They represent, in particular, a great contribution to Ohio's deer-hunting heritage, which remains strong today.

Ohio is home to more than 300,000 deer hunters, whose annual expenditures on deer hunting in Ohio exceed $514 million. Following in the tradition of Oliver Hazard Perry, Ohio's muzzleloading deer hunt today ranks second in the nation. During the state's eight-day muzzleloading season in 1997-98, about 108,000 hunters killed more than 13,000 deer, a state record.

In Perry's diary, we learn that he enjoyed nothing more than a "protracted encampment" with his deer hunting partners. This included a law student named Curtiss; David W. Cross, a New York lawyer; Leonard Case Jr., a Yale lawyer; and his brother William Case, who eventually became mayor of Cleveland.

Perry's deer camps were often the center and rendezvous for extensive deer hunts in all directions for him and his friends. Deer camp camaraderie, however, was not indispensable to Perry.

Charles W. Bingham once wrote: "It was not an uncommon occurrence for him to start out solitary and alone upon one of his great hunts, occupying several months, relying for society — where none intrudes — only upon nature as she always appeared to him in her multitudinous charms." Bingham — a relative, Yale graduate and one-time trustee of Cleveland's Western Reserve Historical Society — described Perry as "an extraordinary and interesting man" who took a keen interest in masculine and physical culture. He was one of America's finest, premier deerslayers, and he exuded class.

"Endowed with a robust constitution, his native tastes and liberal studies inclined him to pursuits of natural history," Bingham wrote.

Perry's intimate knowledge of the whitetail undoubtedly came from experience, but his knowledge of the animal's anatomical detail and life history came from popular natural histories. These works included Richard Harlan's *Fauna Americana* (1825), John D. Godman's *American Natural History* (1826-28), and Audubon and Bachman's *The Quadrupeds of North America* (1851). His passion for hunting white-tailed bucks was also enhanced by reading Alfred B. Street's poem "Deer Shooting," published in

1847, which Perry recited with fondness:

But hark to that sound stealing faint through the wood!
Heart hammers, breath thickens, swift rushes the blood!
It swells from the thicket more loud and more near
'Tis the hound giving tongue! he is driving the deer!
My rifle is levell'd — swift tramplings are heard —
A rustle of leaves — then, with flight like a bird,
His antlers thrown back, and his body in motion
With quick rise and fall like a surge of the ocean —
His eyeballs wide rolling in phrensied affright —
Outbursts the magnificent creature to sight.
A low cry I utter; he stops — bends his head,
His nostrils distended, limbs quaking with dread;
My rifle cracks sharp — he springs wildly on high,
Then pitches down headlong, to quiver and die.

In the evenings after long days of rigorous hunting, Perry and his companions consumed large quantities of hickory nuts and thorn apples. With the aid of a gallon of "Old Jamaica Rum," incidents of deer-camp life translated themselves into legends.

With no alarm clock, these deerslayers occasionally depended on an old veteran rooster from a local farmhouse. Perry wrote, "This crowing of the old Game-Cock of the wilderness was the morning revelry for all hands to muster forth for duty."

Breakfast consisted of fried venison and a cup of spice bush tea. Venison was the staple of these deer hunters. As they roamed the hemlock forest, they continually hung venison in trees. In one of his journal entries, Perry wrote that he "found some venison hanging in a tree, took one Ham and left stuck in a crotched stick a quarter of a dollar for it."

At the first ray of light, they "bent their course" through fields and thickets. Perry describes how David W. Cross, that zealous disciple of Nimrod, headed for the forest:

"Cross put a good quantity of his favorite 'bald

Mr. Edwards in his Hunting Costume.

Oliver Hazard Perry's deer hunting companions — D.W. Cross, above right, a lawyer from New York and "Big" Sam Edwards, left, from Ohio.

eye' in his stomach, a few bullets in his pocket, shouldered his rifle, and turning over with ecstatic delight an old 'chaw' of tobacco in his mouth, started into the woods, the sound of his footsteps reverberating back the exhilarated state of his mind and body."

Perry hunted deer with judges, lawyers, physicians, merchants, landlords, shoemakers, blacksmiths, wealthy farmers, country clerks, hotel keepers and a Scottish cabinetmaker. One historical source reports he even hunted whitetails with "Big" Sam Edwards, an Ohio frontier farmer turned deerslayer, who also wrote *The Ohio Hunter: Or a Brief Sketch of the Frontier Life of Samuel E. Edwards the Great Bear and Deer Hunter of the State of Ohio* (1866).

Perry and Edwards hunted deer in the beautiful terrain and fertile fields of the Maumee River Valley near Napoleon, Ohio. They frequently stayed at the Old Log Tavern in Napoleon, situated between the Erie Canal and Maumee River in Henry County in western Ohio. At the Old Log Tavern, built by George Stout in 1835, the two deer stalkers imbibed in "Native Ohio" and deer-camp discourse.

As with Perry's rigorous, warfare-like deer hunting campaigns, hunts by big Sam Edwards, "the great deer hunter" in Ohio, lasted for months. When they ended, this backwoods deerslayer returned with 30 to 50 deer. Edwards lived off the land as he hunted, and liked nothing better than a good-old, violent brawl with a wounded buck. Oblivious to time, Edwards tramped the forests for miles each day, shot deer in the moonlight, and slept wherever he found himself.

The principal diet of these deerslayers was crude and similar: While Perry consumed generous portions of hickory nuts, thorn apples and snake-root whiskey, Edwards wrote that he ate "corn-mush fried in grease, and full of worms at that." As a result of such diets, Edwards and Perry suffered many attacks of what Perry called "Delirium tremens."

As with Edwards, Perry loved sleighing through the wintry woods to pick up deer with

Western Reserve Historical Society

his horse-drawn cutter, especially on moonlit nights, and then on to Beebee's Tavern on the South Ridge.

Perry became intoxicated with the chase. He tracked bucks for days before returning to camp. Like all hunter-naturalists, he originally studied deer to hunt them and then eventually hunted deer to study them.

On a deer hunt beginning Nov. 24, 1837, Perry joined Cross, Colonel Williams, William Case and five other deerslayers in his little tent in the deer forest of Russia Township in Lorain County. Perry felt at home there, for his father and grandfather were early explorers along the county's Black River. Further, his uncle, Horatio Perry, still lived in Wellington.

"Our Fire Arms consisted of Nine Rifles and Six Pistols, two of them Rifle barreled," Perry wrote in his journal. "Game was not very plenty, but having a good stock of Tobacco, Cigars, Hard Bread, Rum, Brandy, Sugar, and Codfish, we passed the time away merrily. Our Camp was so far in the woods, that we could hear no noise from the settlements, and the dead silence that reigned around at Night,

Adirondack Museum, Blue Mountain Lake, N.Y.

Still Hunting on First Snow: A Second Shot, A.F. Tait, 1855. Like all hunter-naturalists, Perry first studied deer to hunt them and eventually hunted them to study them.

was only broken by the hooting of Owls, and the nasal twang of Cross's singing."

Despite scarce deer and no snow, this five-week expedition produced nine whitetails, three raccoons, one turkey and eight ruffed grouse.

In 1838, William Scrope (1772-1852), published his book *The Art of Deer Stalking*, which Perry read with great delight. Later that year, while writing in his diary Dec. 1, Perry described himself as a "Deer Horns" collector, a man who passionately collected unusual sheds and interlocked antlers. An oil-painting portrait of Perry supports that description.

Perry was one of America's first collectors of antlers and deer-hunting memorabilia, setting the tradition for such modern-day antler collectors as Fred Goodwin of Maine and Phil Schlegel and Widmer Smith of Wisconsin. One can only imagine what Perry would have said had he seen what a railroad engineer spotted about a century later near Windham, Ohio, in the heart of Perry's deer-hunting bailiwick. This is where Ohio's famous Hole-In-The-Horn Buck, was found dead along the tracks. The buck's antlers, perhaps the world's most famous white-tailed deer rack, now have a trade value exceeding $200,000.

After traveling for days over corduroy roads, tree roots and deep, black mud, Perry spent days preparing his camps and deer-hunting shanties. That's not surprising when recalling that his autumn deer hunts lasted two or three months in the North's vast wilderness. Perry usually built three-sided sheds with a roof and open front. To make the roof waterproof, he cut dry cedar bark and lapped each piece over the other like laying oak shingles. Over the bark roof he placed hemlock brush. He kept everything in place by laying poles over the hemlock brush. He chinked the side walls with moss. Perry's deer-hunting shanties resembled those made by early voyageurs, as depicted in Ken Laager's oil-on-canvas painting, *Hunter's Fire* (1989).

Building these primitive shanties and getting to them often proved as adventurous as the chase itself. These backwoods shanties dotted the whitetail's territory across America, and eventually served as quarters for Civil War troops.

After a two-year absence from one of his deer-shanties, and while studying its ruins, Perry reflected on the meaning of deer camp:

"Sad and gloomy thoughts came into my mind when I viewed the well-known trees and other objects, and witnessed the wild desolation, that deep and solemn silence. Here two years before, a happy party of us, in the springtime of our existence, spent a portion of the most pleasant period of our lives. All was life and animation. The noise of singing, laughing, talking, and hooting made the woods resound. But now how different! The great changer Time had intervened, and a part of that merry Company were scattered to all portions of the earth, while two of them were then gazing in melancholy silence on the ruins of their old deserted Camp before them."

While pursuing the "old hemlock rangers," Perry often lived in deserted Indian camps if one of his more permanent shanties wasn't near. He also competed for whitetails with the Potawatomi, Chippewa and Saginaw. Owls were often his only companions as he nestled close to the fire on cold, starry nights. He lived on squirrels, venison and turkey. At the end of the day, after running deer trails for miles, he imbibed in Jamaica rum, smoked his pipe and discussed his "deer chases." He described how bucks "unfurled their white flags to the breeze" while talking with his cohorts at backwoods haunts such as Granny Corslet's Tavern, located a few miles from the tri-state juncture of Michigan, Ohio and Indiana.

On Dec. 14, 1842 — while carrying a single-barreled Swinerton rifle, 50 balls to the pound, and a 2-gallon jug of "Native Ohio" that cost 38 cents per gallon — Perry headed for Redington's Tavern with his friend John Williamson. Perry's stays at country taverns were usually but brief breaks in journeys to his backwoods deer-shanties or to other hunter's abodes.

Perry and Williamson had heard about a wolf hunter named Snyder, who "cabined in the Black Swamp," and so they decided to spend a few days hunting with "the rough Old Wolf Hunter himself." They journeyed 90 miles west of Cleveland, traveling three days by horse and buggy to Woodville, a small community on the Portage River in the heart of the Black Swamp. After wandering on foot in the dark through the Black Swamp, the lost and exhausted hunters finally found Snyder's dilapidated one-room shack. Old Snyder invited the bedraggled pair to stay and hunt deer. Their exhausting travel paid dividends. While still-hunting with Snyder, Perry jumped a noble buck with a "perfect brush heap" on its head, and put its lights out. This wide-beamed and palmated 14-pointer with blackened antlers and thick bases remained Perry's greatest whitetail. He called it "Old Buck."

On Oct. 30, 1845, Perry received a new cast-steel, double-barreled rifle from Morgan James, a New York gunmaker. Bored to about .47 caliber, this muzzle loading rifle weighed 11 pounds and

Gambling for the Buck. **John Mix Stanley, 1867. Oil on canvas. Perry frequently competed with the Potowatomi, Chippewa and Saginaw for white-tailed deer. At times, those tribes also competed amongst themselves for white-tailed bucks.**

carried 45 balls to the pound of lead. This rifle gave Perry the luxury of a fast second shot. Eager to test it and suffering with his "usual fall fever for a deer hunt," Perry and David Cross left Cleveland and headed west for Paulding and Henry counties in northwestern Ohio, carrying with them "an extra amount of excitement and pleasure."

On the fifth day of the hunt, Perry encountered a magnificent buck. Despite his determination to elude that dreaded, eternal disease called buck fever — known in Perry's time as "buck ague" — Perry was so afflicted while shooting twice at the great buck. After missing, he exclaimed:

"The buck fever seized me in a moment. I was all shakes and made two foolish shots at the Old Patriarch, who hearing a noise and smelling gunpowder, threw up his head, hoisted his flag,

***The Hunter's Shanty.* Currier and Ives, 1861. Perry enjoyed living in quickly improvised hemlock shanties and eating trout and venison steak after a long day of deer hunting along the banks of the Maumee River.**

gave a snort and bounded away forever from my sight, leaving me to suffer from chagrin and mortification at the results of my two shots."

After experiencing such failures, Perry frequently imbibed stimulating fluid — sometimes "Old Bald Eye" and other times "Native Ohio" — to lighten his heart and become content with the world.

Perry's thoughts on this hunt transcend 150 years to speak to American deer hunters today. Modern hunters also seek a quality experience by "being alone with others" in the wilderness. While on that 1845 deer hunt, Perry and Cross hunted several days along Ohio's Maumee River, hunting alone during the day and enjoying deer camp camaraderie around the evening fire. One morning, while canoeing the Maumee at daybreak, they stopped and stepped into a large, unexplored forest.

"A strange feeling of solitude came over our minds," Perry wrote in his journal, "and wishing to commune alone with our feelings while pen-

Adirondack Museum, Blue Mountain Lake, N.Y.

etrating the wilderness before us, we parted, and in our course slightly diverged from each other."

Following in the tradition of such deerslayers as Philip Tome of Pennsylvania, Meshach Browning of Maryland, and William Elliott of South Carolina, Perry often found himself with knife in hand in direct contact with struggling bucks. While hunting along the Maumee, Perry heard a noise behind him. Looking that way, he saw a buck dashing toward him. At the report of Perry's new double-barreled rifle, the buck hugged its tail and vanished into dense brush. Perry hastily pursued the track, and within 200 feet suddenly confronted the distressed monarch:

"Rushing up to it, it imploringly cast upon me its green glassy eyes, but regardless of its life pleadings, I drew from its sheath the dreaded steel of 'Sa-con-da-ga,' and plunging it into the throat of the struggling victim, let out the crimson current of its body, as a propitious offering to 'Bow-waw-nee,' the hunters' god."

Perry's knife once belonged to the celebrated Ottawa Chief "Sa-con-da-ga." An old wolf hunter named John Glass opened the grave of this legendary chief in 1838, and took the knife. He later presented it to Perry as a gift.

At the end of this 1845 deer hunting excursion to the Maumee River, which lasted about three weeks, Perry stood on the riverbank "and bid the old echoing woods farewell, determined that the wild denizens that roamed in them, should no more that fall be alarmed by the Cuyahogian Hunter stalking through their forests."

In his thrilling adventures and captivating diaries, the Cuyahogian Hunter captures the romance of the early 19th-century deerslayer. From 1836 to 1855, Perry studied and observed the whitetail. This meant exploring new terrain; canoeing rivers on moonlit nights; chopping beech trees for exercise, and then carving his signature into the wood; cooking and eating venison tenderloins in front of a campfire; sleeping on aromatic beds of hemlock boughs after listening to owl hoots, deer snorts,

Stag's Head. A.F. Tait, 1852. Like Tait, Perry maintained a passion for pursuing white-tailed deer.

Adirondack Museum, Blue Mountain Lake, N.Y.

wolf howls and elk bugles; and spending rainy days reading sporting literature in quaint country taverns that often served as local post offices.

Oliver Hazard Perry died in a railroad accident while hunting deer near Earlville on Dec. 23, 1864, at age 47. In an article published in *Forest and Stream*, Perry's deer-hunting comrade David W. Cross paid homage to him, writing that Perry "lived long enough to achieve unrivaled fame as a hunter, and such a remembrance in the hearts of his friends, of his noble, generous and unselfish character that no lapse of time can ever obliterate."

There is indeed a timelessness to Perry's deer hunts that transcends the centuries. His romantic and adventurous experiences — and his intimate quest for details of deer behavior — still evoke familiar awe in all lovers of the chase.

Au

CAMPING ON THE
U SABLE

Michigan Historical Collection. Bentley Historical Library, University of Michigan.

"The first evening in camp around the council-lamp was spent in discussing the prospects of the morrow and in shooting over again all the deer that had been shot upon previous occasions."

— W. M. Laffin,
"Deer Hunting On the Au Sable."
Scribner's Monthly, April 1878.

Oliver Hazard Perry died in a railroad accident on the Cleveland & Pittsburgh Railroad on Dec. 23, 1864, while returning from a deer hunt in Michigan's Upper Peninsula. Had he lived longer, he might have visited Deer Camp Erwin in Iosco County near Oscoda, Mich., along the banks of the Au Sable River, whose waters were the color of dark-brown sherry. During the height of the lumbering era, this deer camp consisted of a rickety barn, a broken-down blacksmith shop and a well-ventilated house of log construction. Just how well-ventilated Deer Camp Erwin actually was, we learn from the memoirs of a camp resident:

"The ventilation of the deer shack was generous in the extreme. The roof was tight, but all around one found open chinks between the logs; through these the stars could be seen by anybody that had nothing better to do than look at them. Up through the middle of the floor and out through a big hole at the ridge-pole went the stove pipe, always hot enough to worry an insurance man."

The residents of this deer camp slept on ticks filled with straw, which were laid on the floor. Because their consciences were always clear (a normal situation for most deer hunters), they slept with exceeding soundness. Some dreamt of giant bucks, others of rifles that wouldn't go off.

During the gun season of 1877, Sept. 15 through Dec. 15, and ever since 1859 when Michigan initiated its first regulated deer season, 12 mighty hunters of the wilderness lived there. While in camp, they ate vast quantities of venison and "bedewed" the deer shack floor, pleasantly and copiously, with infusions of Virginia plug.

During mid-October 1877, 12 gentlemen from all walks of life came from great distances to meet on an appointed day in Bay City at the head of Saginaw Bay. From there, they took a steamer to Tawas, where they spent the night at a backwoods tavern called the Buck House and enjoyed a vast quantity of broiled venison. From Tawas, horse-drawn wagons and sleighs took them 26 miles farther through the great wasteland of scrub oaks and stout Norway pines to the famed deer-hunting grounds of the Au Sable and legendary Deer Camp Erwin, an old deserted logging camp.

At 4:30 each morning, these deer hunters were awakened by boss man Erwin, who shouted, "Daylight in the swamp!" The hunters slowly arose from their straw-filled mattresses and made their way to the first floor, where they found frying pans filled with sizzling rashers of bacon and pots of hot coffee in full blast — the aroma doing

George Shiras III. National Geographic Society.

justice to upscale restaurants. After a short trip to the two-holer, they returned to a hearty meal of bacon, venison liver, boiled potatoes, fried onions, and bread and butter.

"The fragrance that filled the air of the cabin surpassed the most delicate vapors that ever escaped from one of Delmonico's covers," a New York visitor insisted. This visitor, W.M. Laffin, believed the cabin's fragrance and the air of the

Horse-drawn sleighs took members of Deer Camp Erwin through the great wilderness of scrub oaks and stout Norway pines to the famed deer-hunting grounds of the Au Sable River.

Au Sable could be marketed in New York City for incredible sums of money.

In his essay on this camp in the April 1878 issue of *Scribner's Monthly*, Laffin wrote: "Coats were then buttoned up, rubber blankets and ammunition belts slung over shoulders, cartridge maga-

Courtesy of Rob Wegner's Photo Collection.

OUR CAPTAIN.

This illustration by W.M. Laffin of John Erwin — known in deer camp as "Our Captain" — appeared in the April 1878 issue of *Scribner's Monthly*.

zines filled, hatchets stuck into belts, rifles shouldered and out we sallied into the darkness through which the faintest glimmer of gray was just showing in the east."

Thus armed with high hopes, the rugged woodsmen of Deer Camp Erwin headed for their early-morning stands in the deep thickets of Cedar Swamp with Winchester rifles in hand. Cedar Swamp, a well-known landmark, consisted of a narrow belt of low bottomlands on each side of the Au Sable, with giant cedars growing to the water's edge.

Nowhere on Earth, at least for the first few hours in the depths of Cedar Swamp, did hope bloom so eternal. Then a steadily falling, freezing rain soon changed the picture to a somewhat uncomfortable state, where hands became numb and teeth chattered like "miniature castanets." Still, they refused to put on their heavy gloves for fear they would hamper their shooting ability. As the day passed they stamped their feet and did the "London cabman's exercise" with hands and arms to keep warm. Distant shots frequently reverberated through the forest.

At camp that night, the lucky hunters had to tell again and again how they shot big bucks of the 250-pound variety. Laffin referred to the language used in these deer camp tales as "native windiness." No one ever shot a small deer! No such thing existed.

"We could not meet a man in the country all about that had ever seen a small deer. The word fawn, from desuetude, will be dropped from their language. It was always the blankest, biggest buck! blank me! or the blank, blankest blank of a blank of a blank doe running like blank and blankation for the blank river! That was all we could ever get, and when perchance one of these identical, peculiarly qualified animals happened to be shot, the speaker stood wholly unabashed and unconscious in the presence of his refutation. It must be in the climate."

Most deer hunters who hung out at Deer Camp Erwin used the Winchester Model 1873 carbine in .44-40 caliber — the rifle Jimmy Stewart immortalized in the movie *Winchester '73*. Most of them agreed with T.S. Van Dyke about this rifle: "The combined ingenuity of Earth, even assisted by light from on high, could not improve upon the quintessence of perfection for deer hunting known as the Winchester of '73."

All deer camps need a boss man in residence, and Deer Camp Erwin was no exception. John Erwin of Cleveland, Ohio — a gentleman at whose door lay the death of a grievous quantity of big-racked bucks — fit the bill. From one account we learn that his 70 years "imparted rigor and activity to his stalwart and symmetrical frame." This account went on to say of

John Erwin, holding his Winchester Model '73, proudly displays his 250-pound field-dressed buck, which he shot in burnings near the Au Sable. Forest fires frequently swept the area.

Michigan Historical Collection, Bentley Historical Library, University of Michigan.

Courtesy of Rob Wegner's Photo Collection.

Erwin: "Hale, hearty, capable of enduring all manner of fatigue, unerring with his Winchester rifle, full of the craft of the woods, and an inexhaustible fund of kindly humor, he was the soul of our deer camp. All twelve hunters were under his orders, and remained so until the deer hunt was over." According to one visiting deer hunter, "He was implicitly obeyed; none of his orders were unpleasant; they simply implied the necessary discipline of successful deer camp hunting."

Their cherished method of deer hunting involved placing 10 standers with Winchesters at named and well-established deer crossings and runways along the Au Sable, while two hunters and the dogs took up the track to move deer toward the water. The standers frequently shot as the fleeing deer swam the Au Sable — a practice the Michigan Legislature outlawed in 1881.

In his account of Deer Camp Erwin, Laffin wrote that John Erwin and his boys were reading John Dean Caton's book *The Deer and Antelope of America* (1877), and derived their knowledge of deer behavior and anatomy from it. They prided themselves on Caton's measure of what a deer hunt is all about. We see here the appearance of the essence of sportsmanship in the late 1870s:

"The pleasure of the sportsman in the chase is measured by the intelligence of the game and its capacity to elude pursuit and in the labor involved in the capture. It is a contest with sharp wits where satisfaction is mingled with admiration for the object overcome."

When considering Caton's many deer hunting trips to the Au Sable, and his voluminous letter correspondence with Laffin and many Michigan sportsmen, it seems likely Caton hunted deer at Deer Camp Erwin in the late 1870s.

They also read deer hunting articles in *The American Field*, *The American Sportsman*, *The Chicago Field* and the popular *Forest and Stream*, edited by Charles Hallock. One two-part article

In his painting *Bringing Home Game: Winter Shanty at Ragged Lake*, 1856, A.F. Trait captured the spirit of early deer hunting shanties, whether located in the Adirondacks or the land of Hiawatha.

CAMPING ON THE AU SABLE   37

Courtesy of Rob Wegner's Photo Collection.

titled "Deer Hunting In Michigan," published in *Forest and Stream* in 1877, was written by "Greenhorn," the pen name for C.E. Anderson, a contributor to the rod-and-gun column of the *New York Sun*. Camp members discussed Greenhorn's article at length, for it provided a classic description of hunting whitetails along the Au Sable with dogs and Winchesters during the height of Michigan's lumbering era. In the fireplace's dim light, Laffin read, reread and quoted this literary gem to his companions:

Deer carcasses await shipment to the South on the Grand Rapids & Indiana Railways at Mackinaw City, Mich. Carcasses arrived at the depot by the wagonload during the late 1800s.

"I wait in the grand solitude of the virgin forest, with ears intent for the voice of the hounds. I cannot tell how long I waited. I only know that in a supreme moment of contemplation, when the soul seemed filled with the greatness, the grandeur, the glory of the illimitable wilderness, I was suddenly aroused to a realizing sense of the situation by a distant cry of the hounds, distant and low at first, gradually coming nearer and more distinct; now evidently running to the north, now to the south. Oh! the music of that full chorus, which now began to break loudly on the still air, was inspiring. All else was still as death, every particular hair was standing on end with expectation.

"A'ah! there is a commotion in the brush over by that stump. A crash in the thicket and out rushes like the wind an old gray-haired monarch, plunging like lightning right by my wondering and bewildered vision, and myself powerless to raise an arm to stop him. In an instant, however, Richard Greenhorn is himself again, and I send a wild shot after him. He is away now two-hundred yards, going straight from me. I raise my Winchester again with comparative deliberation this time. Ah! Old fellow, where are you now? His heels fly up, and turning a complete somersault he lies still. The shot had struck him behind the ear and entered his brain, and in falling his momentum had carried him completely over."

The midday dinner at Deer Camp Erwin consisted of a larded saddle of venison flanked by a dish of steaming bacon and cabbage, plus vast quantities of potatoes and fried onions. The evening supper also turned into a backwoods venison extravaganza. After supper, Erwin's boys returned to the woods with lanterns in hand to retrieve the dead and wounded deer shot during the day. One practice entailed finding dead deer in the magnificent light of blazing birch bark.

"As we made our way along the bank, our back-woodsman would pick out here and there a large white birch, and apply a match to the curling ringlets of bark at the foot of its trunk. In a minute the whole stem of the tree was in a roaring blaze that lit up the riverbank all round about and made the great cedars look like gigantic skeletons. Each birch was a brilliant spectacle, while it burned in a crackling, sparkling column of flame, sending showers of sparks through the forest, and then dying out in an angry red and a cloud of murky smoke."

On the seventh day of the 1877 hunt, with 12 deer hanging in the barn, Laffin admitted he felt guiltless of the death of any of them. He returned with high hopes to his appointed deer stand along the Au Sable in the heart of Cedar Swamp. He soon heard a shot near the river and the baying of hounds. Suddenly, a large buck appeared in the shallow water before him.

"He was a stalwart, thick-set fellow; his legs were short and compact, his fur was dark in its winter hue, and his antlers glistened above his head. He bore himself proudly as he stood in the water and turned to listen for the bay of the dogs he had outrun. I hesitated a moment, doubtful if I should let him get into the stream and swim down, or shoot at him as he stood. I chose the latter, aimed quietly and confidently, and fired. He pitched forward, the current seized him, and he floated down with it and past me, dead."

In deciding not to shoot the buck while swimming, we see the emerging essence of sportsmanship. By the time Laffin returned to camp, their guide, Curtis, had retrieved the buck and already hung it in the barn. After receiving acclamations from his fellow hunters, measurements were taken, and Laffin's buck was granted the place of honor at the head of the line. Merriment and songs followed, with sundry snatches of the Forester's Chorus from *As You Like It*:

"What shall he have that killed the deer?"

By the time the 12 hunters broke camp in mid-December 1877, 23 deer hung on the meatpole in the barn. Laffin's trophy buck remained at the head of the line. The hunt had been successful in more ways than one. No one got lost, and no visitor left camp hungry or thirsty. The hunters paid well for local services, and treated local people with courtesy. Indeed, the hunters at Deer Camp Erwin developed a long-lasting friendship with local loggers and farmers. After a rough ride aboard horse-drawn wagons, the hunters boarded a train for Detroit. Along the way, they enjoyed a leisurely meal with cigars and whiskey. They arrived in Detroit with about 3,000 pounds of venison. After saying their farewells to each other, they went their individual ways, thus ending an "expedition with plenty of wholesome recreation to make one's recollection of it wholly pleasant."

The E.C. Nichols Deer Hunting Camps along the Au Sable several miles west of Deer Camp Erwin on the South Branch of the Au Sable also provide pleasant recollections of early American deer camps. One of the earliest deer hunting pictures in existence shows the E.C. Nichols Deer Camp in 1876 near Ball's Bridge. The camp featured everything from ties and suit coats to chinaware and table cloths.

Although it's difficult in that era to distinguish between shooting deer for sustenance or recreation, by the late 1870s many Americans followed

Michigan hunters pose with whitetails and Winchesters along the Au Sable River in 1877.

Courtesy of Rob Wegner's Photo Collection.

Perry and Erwin and went afield primarily for recreation. Rapid industrialization brought wealth and leisure to more people and thus created opportunities to hunt deer for recreation. The rapid growth of the railroad system brought deer hunters into the heart of the whitetail's territory. Deer hunting, however, did not become the hobby of the butcher, the baker and candlestick maker overnight. That had to wait a generation or more, but for those who could afford it —

such as E.C. Nichols, a prominent manufacturer of threshing machinery in Battle Creek, Mich. — deer hunting became a popular pastime during the late 1870s.

Unlike Laffin's description of Deer Camp Erwin, deer hunters of the 1870s did not diligently chronicle their deer-camp experiences for posterity. In reconstructing early deer-camp experiences, we rely on an occasional sketch or reminiscence found in a more general book on

Michigan Department of State, State Archives.

hunting and fishing. One such account, "A Sketch of the Nichols Deer Hunting Camps," appeared in William B. Mershon's *Recollections of My Fifty Years of Hunting and Fishing* (1923). It was written by Edwin C. Nichols.

From his account, we learn that although some deer hunters like Oliver Hazard Perry insisted on camping inside hollow logs, most deer camps in the 1870s consisted of primitive tents with black, protruding stovepipes belching smoke into the

By the end of the 19th century, tented cities, such as this camp from the 1890s, began to show up in northern Michigan and its Upper Peninsula.

pines. Most also featured a "goodly number of deer in the hangings," as Nichols described it in an unpublished letter to conservationist Mershon.

Their camp in the early years was a rather unpretentious affair when compared to luxurious developments in the later years. They traveled to and from camp with a large lumber

Michigan Historical Collection: Bentley Historical Library, University of Michigan.

The Hanging of the Deer. Oil painting by Courtier. Hiram T. Merill, left, of Johnstown, Mich., and John Nichols of Battle Creek, Mich., hang a buck near the Au Sable River in Autumn 1876.

wagon and a pair of horses. Their deer camp never lacked grand food. Venison prevailed as the choice meat. To this primitive tent on the Au Sable came a small band of deer hunters each year armed with muzzleloading rifles. These die-hard muzzleloaders hunted with dogs.

"Any true sportsman who has on a keen, frosty, early morning listened to the music of one or two loud baying hounds following the wily buck in full swing will not soon forget the electric thrill that the chase brings to every hunter within hearing; each hoping the deer is headed for his stand and with every sense acute, every muscle tense, he listens to the echoes and re-echoes of the baying dogs as they follow on the track of the flying deer."

Year by year, the E.C. Nichols deer camp increased its hospitable features. The camp soon included a large cooking and dining tent with a solid oak floor, an oak dining room table with white tablecloth and napkins, modern chinaware and table silver, a large cooking stove, comfortable chairs, a hot water reservoir, large pancake griddle, and sleeping tents with comfortable bedding and a commissary tent for storage of all provisions. The

camp also had auxiliary tents for extra guests. It was not uncommon for the camp to have more than 20 deer hunters in attendance for more than 40 days. The importance of these deer camps and the hospitality of its founder, E.C. Nichols, were heralded in sporting journals of the day.

The party traveled by rail to Roscommon, and then down the South Branch of the Au Sable with 10 purebred deer hounds, all loaded into five large scows:

"They went gaily sailing down that beautiful stream on a bright October day. The South Branch at that time was densely wooded with overhanging trees along the margin, and grand strips of Norway and white pine bordering it. It was a fine rushing torrent down which the boats sped with little effort, except to dodge the overhanging sweepers and clear the treacherous whirlpools."

This deer camp had every attraction of location and surroundings, plus a great abundance of white-tailed deer and the companionship of family and friends gathered on its shores. E.C. Nichols described the site:

"Our favorite hunting camp site, and one which we occupied for several successive years, was on the north bank of the river a few miles below where the North Branch joins its rushing waters with the majestic main stream of the Au Sable. It was a beautiful hillside crowned with a grove of stately Norway pines, sloping gently down to the water's edge, forming a delightful frontage looking up stream. When our Tented City was in full regalia on this beautiful hillside, it presented a very interesting and charming picture as one rounded the river bend above and came into full view."

In the warm and secure atmosphere of their tented city, the E.C. Nichols hunters read *The Chicago Field*, a leading sportsman's journal. Of particular interest were the so-called "Brompton Papers," a series of in-depth articles written under the logo "Camp Life Memories" by John J. Brompton, a popular Indiana deerslayer/writer. Sounding at times like Oliver Hazard Perry, Brompton entertained his readers with his wild deer hunts in Michigan's Upper Peninsula, where his buddy Turkey Frank eventually killed the great monarch of the glen. Brompton's deer-hunting epistles were read and quoted as deer camp scripture:

> *A mellow mist hangs on the trees,*
> *A weird song floats on the breeze;*
> *The night-bird hoots his doleful note*
> *In answer to the lone coyote.*
> *The moonlight falls in splendor bright*
> *Upon our tent this Autumn night.*

The annual Nichols deer camps continued for many years, mostly on the Au Sable River and its tributaries. Photos of these deer camps depict the features of their forest homes, and also suggest the many pleasures and comforts to be found in deer camp.

When Michigan outlawed hounds for deer hunting in 1887, the E.C. Nichols Deer Hunting Camps formally suspended operations. These die-hard muzzleloaders could not accept the outlawing of hounds nor the development of the repeating rifle. They hung up their rifles and stored their equipment, but the memory of their camps and their happy days afield remains gratefully and lovingly cherished in the annals of American deer hunting.

W.M. Laffin's romantic illustration of Deer Camp Erwin, which appeared in the April 1878 issue of *Scribner's Monthly*.

CAMP ERWIN.

Courtesy of Rob Wegner's Photo Collection.

HITEFISH
LAKE DEER CAMP

An Anxious Moment, A.F. Tait, 1880. Adirondack Museum. Blue Mountain Lake, N.Y.

"A sportsman's life consists largely of three elements: anticipation, realization and reminiscence. We look forward to the trip by rail, by canoe and then perhaps a tramp on foot into the heart of the wilderness. Then comes the camp and its pleasant environments, and that lucky, radiant day when the early-morning sun casts a glint upon the branching antlers of a mighty buck."

— George Shiras III,
National Geographic,
July 1906

In 1870, John Bush of Ohio shot his world-class 14-pointer in Minnesota. It measured 181⅛ typical, and still ranks as the second oldest whitetail in the Boone and Crockett Club's *Records of North American Big Game*. That same year, an American Indian deer hunting guide named Jack La Pete — known in the Lake Superior region as the "Jack of Spades," because he looked like the Jack of Spades — guided a boy on a two-day deer hunt to a small, beautiful lake in a virgin forest about 20 miles southeast of Marquette in Alger County of Michigan's Upper Peninsula. (Alger is currently one of the top 10 counties for entries in the *Commemorative Bucks of Michigan Inc.* record book.)

After bringing down his first white-tailed buck on that trip, the 11-year-old boy, George Shiras III (1859-1942), named the place Whitefish Lake. It was there that Shiras, shortly before the E.C. Nichols Deer Camp suspended operations, established the Whitefish Lake Deer Camp, which

George Shiras III (1859-1942) was the founding father of wildlife photography and the legendary Whitefish Lake Deer Camp in Michigan.

The Marquette County Historical Society, Marquette, Mich.

became the wilderness headquarters for the father of deer photography. His famous deer and deer hunting photos of the 1880s remain unsurpassed in quality, clarity and composition.

Shiras, who was destined to become a member of the United States Congress, also went on to become a sporting friend of Theodore Roosevelt. In an essay published in *National Geographic* magazine in 1906, Shiras described his first encounter with Whitefish Lake: "A glance to the north disclosed a narrow lake about a mile long, heavily forested along its shore with pine and hemlock, except at the end, where a growth of reeds, backed by cedars and black ash, indicated the outlet stream. To the south, a beautiful bay, or slough, lay between high hills, with reeds, water lilies, and sandy beaches at the end, through which the inlet stream issued from a gorge filled, as far as vision reached, with stately elms. This was the center of fine deer country."

Shiras returned to this secluded hideaway for more than 60 consecutive years in his never ending pursuit of the white-tailed deer. Deer camp aficionados will find his brilliant autobiographical account of this deer camp, as well as his adventures with the area's whitetails, in his two-volume work titled, *Hunting Wild Life with Camera and Flashlight* (1935).

The earliest permanent deer camp at Whitefish Lake was a crude affair in 1882. The bark-roofed structure went through a long series of improvements that eventually culminated in a compound of modern buildings in 1895. The camp was complete with boat house, caretaker's quarters, and a large family dwelling. A log cabin for guests, such as deer hunter A.O. Jopling, was built in 1886. In a classic deer camp photo of the time, A.O. Jopling proudly displays his extraordinary, large-bodied white-tailed buck and his cherished, well-worn Winchester Model 1873.

By the turn of the century, the Shiras deer camp included barns, poultry houses, an ice house, a maple-sugar plant that annually produced 500 gallons of syrup, a saw mill that produced timber for various improvements, primitive deer shacks scattered throughout the area, and a camp garden that produced 27 varieties of vegetables. Besides the garden's produce, Shiras writes: "There were strawberries, raspberries, blackberries, currants and gooseberries, a few cherries and a considerable orchard of apples. A rock and water garden indicated that the eye as well as the stomach had received attention."

Five generations of the Shiras family hunted deer at this secluded retreat. In 1927, they built a 9-foot fence to keep deer out!

In 1882, Shiras' early transportation from the railroad to the Whitefish Lake Deer Camp involved a "wild, merry sleigh ride" through dense timber and swamps, with frequent stops to blaze the trail. Shiras' passion for these primitive backwoods retreats reveals itself in his photos. In fact, these photographs constitute some of the greatest artifacts in the history of white-tailed deer hunting in America.

Who would deny the wildness and primitive character of Jack La Pete's deer hunting abode? He lived in this deer shack while guiding the Shiras family on deer hunts for three generations.

We would have to call the Peter White Deer Camp on Whitefish Lake the ultimate lap of luxury. In 1884, a roof had just been built over the table in front of the original lean-to.

Peter White — Shiras' father-in-law and one of the early developers of the Upper Peninsula's ore, lumber and shipping industries — saw to it that bucks arrived at camp in class aboard a jumper sled. (A jumper is a logging sled with a high crosspiece that supported the log's forward end while dragging its back end.) When the sleds arrived, the Shiras meat pole was filled to capacity. In his caption for a photo titled "Two Bucks Were Brought In On A Jumper," Shiras wrote: "The transformation of the forest by its first mantle of white always gave a peculiar exhilaration to our deer hunts."

Shiras loved to hunt whitetails from White's crude retreat. His early deer hunting adventures

National Geographic Society.

George Shiras III brings two does and an 8-point buck back to camp in a skiff, 1887.

revolved around jacklighting deer on Whitefish Lake. This tactic was generally considered a legitimate hunting method during the 1870s and 1880s. On his first adventure in jacklighting — or fire-hunting as they commonly called it — young Shiras sat in a dugout canoe made from a white pine log. As this backwoods deerslayer followed the Whitefish Lake shoreline in the canoe, his guide and canoe companion, Jake Brown, maintained a fire in an old frying pan. The pan contained a handful of pine knots, to which he added strips of burning birch bark when more light was needed. Suddenly, Brown whispered to his young tenderfoot, "Put up your rifle, there's a deer ahead."

Shiras shares what happened next:

"At first I could neither see nor hear one, but after passing some reeds bordering a little bay, I saw, standing within less than 30 yards, a small buck, intently feeding on the succulent water plants growing a few inches below the surface.

"Silently I raised my gun and aimed for the shoulder. As the black smoke and heavy report evidenced the pulling of the trigger, the deer gave a spasmodic whirl and rushed toward the shore at an extraordinary speed, the water flying in all directions. Once more I fired, just as the animal, in a single leap, cleared the first bushes and disappeared.

"Reverberating echoes from the high ground across the lake did not drown Jake's chuckle; but he gave assurance of another shot within an hour.

"Another shot!! What a mockery this seemed to one who felt sure that this first-time effort had been successful. If not, what chance would there ever be of doing better?

"With assumed confidence, therefore, I insisted that we should find the deer dead within a short distance. But Jake only laughed and steered the canoe toward the opposite shore. It was evidently his opinion that buck fever had given my prey a further lease on life."

That night, the disappointed Shiras resolved to rise at daybreak with the faint hope of finding the

deer. The next morning, he pushed his canoe off without disturbing the others, and headed for the marsh where he had shot at the deer. The dry mud soon gave evidence of where the buck had gone ashore. Pushing his canoe into the brush, he leaped clear of the muddy shoreline and grabbed a protruding snag for support. To his surprise, the protruding snag turned out to be the hind leg of his dead buck.

Shiras sank to the ground trembling with emotion. A thorough examination indicated nine buckshot pellets had passed through the body, piercing the heart and lungs. This instance demonstrated to the young hunter how far a deer can run even when mortally wounded. The fact

Larry Huffman/Legendary Whitetails Collection.

that most deer indicate by their actions the effect and probable location of a hit remained cloudy for 1880s jacklighters.

The Whitefish Lake Deer Camp log indicates that every night the hunters sat around the fire and listened to Shiras' deer hunting yarns as flames leaped and sparks danced into the trees. By the late 1870s, Shiras and his partners had read the popular book *Floating and Driving for Deer* by James Low Jr., and recalled the stirring events of fire-hunting whitetails as described by Low. They also read A.B. Street's poem, "Floatin' for Deer," first published in *The American Sportsman* on Dec. 2, 1872, and set to music by James Ballard of New York in 1873.

Aided by Shiras' musical talents, the crew sang stanzas from the great poem until the wee hours of the evening:

> *The woods are all sleeping, the midnight is dark;*
> *We launch on the still wave our bubble-like bark;*
> *The rifle all ready, the jack burning clear,*
> *And we brush through the lily-pads, floating for deer,*
> *Floating for deer.*
> *And we glide o'er the shallow, boys, floating for deer.*

Philadelphia Museum of Art.

Above, John Bush shot this buck in 1870. It is the second oldest buck in the Boone and Crockett records, scoring 181⅛ typical. Left, *Huntsman and Dogs*. Winslow Homer, oil on canvas, 1891.

Like the young Theodore Roosevelt, Shiras was initially enamored with canoeing at night under the starry, moonlit sky for deer:

"To the straining eye of the one in the bow, intent on the diverging avenue of light cast by the jack-light revolving on its staff, the overhanging branches and the bleached or gnarled trunks assume weird shapes.

"When finally, there was detected the intermittent swish-swish-swish of a deer wading knee-deep in search of tender roots, one tried to pierce the darkness ahead for the first faint glimmer of reflected light from the deer's eyes, which would become brilliant orbs as we approached.

"Then the blue translucent glow of the watching eyes appeared, and as the approaching light revealed the graceful image of a deer, the time to shoot had come. Sometimes the novice, seeing the momentary glow of a firefly or the glistening dew-drop on a reed, imagined he saw a shadowy form and fired at the apparition."

While floating for deer in 1880 in a canoe with Jake Brown on Sixteen-Mile Lake in northern Michigan, Shiras spotted a buck feeding in the shallows along a wooded point. He left the canoe to stalk the buck along the shoreline. Jake soon shouted, "The deer has gone into the water on the other side." Shiras ran across the point with another hunting companion and saw the buck within easy rifle shot, swimming through a bay filled with thick mud.

George Shiras III. National Geographic Society.

Shots burst at once from their repeating Winchester rifles. Bullets ricocheted around the swimming buck, but to no avail. Shiras soon heard his colleague's rifle click, indicating an empty chamber. While hastily looking for more shells himself, he said, "Just watch me knock that old boy over!" His Winchester Model '73 carbine in .44-40 caliber with a 20-inch special octagon barrel barked and barked. The buck's head gradually sank into the water.

"This shows the difference when you take accurate aim!" Shiras shouted.

When this amateurish fusillade ended, old Jake got the young hunters into the canoe and headed for the sinking buck. After pulling the buck to shore, Shiras examined its head, the only part of the deer that had been exposed to the barrage.

"There's not a mark on it other than two bullet holes through the ears," he said with a frown.

On shore, the hunters and their guide cleaned mud from the carcass and examined the entire body, never finding another mark. In a state of

Left, this deer hunting camp in Alger County in Michigan's Upper Peninsula, 1884, belonged to Peter White, George Shiras' father-in-law. Shown here are, from left, Jack La Pete; young Brassey, later Lord Brassey; McLean, a stroke oarsman in the Oxford crew; White; and Charley, a deer hunting guide. Below, the first permanent Whitefish Lake Deer Camp, 1882. Deer hunting guide Jake Brown sits at the table beside the crude, bark-roofed structure.

George Shiras III. National Geographic Society.

amazement and bewilderment, Brown opened the body cavity and remarked, "I know what did this buck in; it died of fright." He showed the two shooters the deer's stomach. It was filled with blood, indicating that in its struggles with the thick mud, the buck ruptured a major blood vessel. The old guide then added to the young hunters' chagrin: "Next time use blank cartridges. The more powder in them the better!"

Shiras never forgot his youthful enthusiasm for floating for white-tailed bucks along the shores of Whitefish Lake. The following passage from an article in the *New York Sun*, dated Aug. 25, 1895, vividly illustrates his passion:

"One beautiful autumn afternoon when but a mere lad, I took my place in the bow of a dugout and was silently paddled along the shore of a little lake sequestered in an almost unbroken wilderness. An aged Sioux hunter acted as my guide and mentor. Soon the quick ear of the Indian detected the indescribable swish-swish-swish of a deer as it waded leisurely through the high reeds on the opposite shore. In a few minutes the declining sun broke out with startling distinctness the half submerged body of a handsome buck as he energetically floundered about in the shallow water in quest of lily pads and succulent water grasses.

"Steadily the canoe drew high across the placid

buck was mud, literally and figuratively. The numerous bullet holes were evidence of marksmanship and skill; the blood-stained reeds and lilies, the streamers and rosettes of victory."

Over time, Shiras began to view jacklighting deer as fatally unfair, and consequently abandoned the practice well before Michigan outlawed it in 1887. As a result of his jacklighting experiences, he had a dramatic fascination with the romantic adventures of surprising deer in their haunts with a sudden direct and revealing light. He eventually devised a flashlight apparatus that enabled him to photograph deer he encountered on his nightly canoe trips.

After several years of mishaps, experimentation and personal frustrations, he developed and patented a hand-held mechanism that fired like a pistol and photographed deer at night. His nighttime photographs of deer taken during cruises around Whitefish Lake remain world-famous. His buck photo titled "Alert!" and his photo, "A Doe and Her Twin Fawns Feeding on a Lake in Northern Michigan," were two of the five famous Midnight Series that won highest awards at the

Below, this photo, titled "Alert!" was taken by George Shiras. Along with "A Doe and Her Twin Fawns Feeding on a Lake in Northern Michigan," left, "Alert" won highest honors in Paris in 1900 and in St. Louis in 1904.

George Shiras III. National Geographic Society.

bay without one interrupting glance from the pronged target so soon to be deprived of the vital spark we treasure so ourselves. The buck fever raged madly in the forecastle of that tiny craft . . . True to the Indian custom, the word 'shoot' never came until the raising head gave notice that we might be seen, so close at hand was the boat. The right barrel belched forth a noisy cloud of gray smoke, concealing from the eager eyes the transverse rain of leaden hail, but the other senses plainly told that few had gone astray. Two dying leaps, and the struggling beast fell in a mass of air white lilies with the life bereft before the echoes of that deadly blast had traversed back to me.

"In my boyish enthusiasm the name of that

Adirondack Museum, Blue Mountain Lake, N.Y.

Paris Exposition in 1900 and the World's Fair in St. Louis in 1904.

Shiras learned that nighttime deer hunting with a camera held greater attraction for an experienced hunter like himself than did hunting with the rifle. He conveyed this information to others through columns in *Forest and Stream*, which was edited by his friend George Bird Grinnell. The dark, warm nights, the smell of magnesium powder in the flashlight apparatus, the gentle ripple of the canoe paddle, the wooded banks wrapped in haunting shadows with only the skyline dimly revealing the hunter's course all enhanced the adventure's romance and mystique. Hoof stamps, snorts, deer struggling and plunging toward the brush all mesmerized these camera hunters.

Suddenly, the form of a majestic buck would appear and the tension would mount. As Shiras wrote in his diary: "There is a click, and a white wave of light breaks out from the bow of the boat — deer, hills, trees — everything stands out for an instant in the white glare of noonday. A dull report, and then a veil of inky darkness descends. What a strange phenomenon! Nothing like it has ever been seen on the lake during the days of its deerhood."

As with Roosevelt, Shiras belonged to the era's leading sportsmen's organizations: the Explorers' Club of New York, the Boone and Crockett Club and the American Game Protective Association. In 1910, these men met at Cornell University to receive honorary doctorates for their field studies in natural history. Shiras was also a leading member of the Huron Mountain Club, a famous Midwestern deer hunting club whose ideals set the tone for sporting ethics across America. Many members of these clubs hunted deer at the Whitefish Lake Deer Camp.

Shiras shot his finest buck one mile west of his deer camp — a 13-pointer with a 25-inch inside spread — on Nov. 17, 1895. This was the year

These hunters prepare for a night of jacklighting for whitetails with Winchester 1873s, circa 1880.

Michigan required its first deer hunting license, which cost 50 cents, and its first state-imposed bag limit of five deer. Shiras' buck weighed 275 pounds when it fell. Its head was on display for many years in his camp's guest cabin above the massive stone fireplace. There it hung alongside other cherished deer-hunting memorabilia of the Shiras family, including famous deer and deer hunting prints by Winslow Homer, Philip R. Goodwin, Carl Rungius and Frederick Remington.

Those who hunted at the Whitefish Lake Deer Camp shared Shiras' belief that the most significant aspect of deer hunting focused on an active role in nature. They maintained an intense involvement with deer in their natural habitat. Deer hunting immersed them in an awareness of natural phenomena organized into a coherent and unified framework. They viewed whitetails with respect and affection. Yet, they participated in that ancient and mysterious contradiction of the hunters' soul, the ultimate paradox: They killed the animal they loved. In deer hunts at Whitefish Lake Deer Camp, they saw the creature at its best: when it's being hunted.

Left, A.O. Jopling of Marquette, Mich., poses with his Winchester Model 1873 and a large-bodied 8-pointer in front of the Whitefish Lake Deer Camp cabin, built in 1886. Below, Jake Brown, one of Shiras' guides, sits in front of Jack La Pete's deer hunting abode.

George Shiras III. National Geographic Society.

George Shiras III, National Geographic Society.

Although born in Pittsburgh's great industrial center, and educated in the eastern Ivy League tradition — Phillips Academy, Cornell and Yale — Shiras hunted deer over virtually every part of the Lake Superior region. From his famous Michigan deer camp, he tramped into the wilderness to hunt, study and observe deer and to photograph their everyday existence. He pursued deer in one way or another for more than 60 years. When his deer camp was generously supplied with venison, the camera offered further means of exercising even greater hunting skill than did rifle hunting. Skill, not kill, became the primary motive in Shiras' deer hunts. Shiras interpreted the latter word in a subordinate sense: The method becomes more important than the material results.

Shiras considered taking a deer's life as "an unavoidable incident in the gratification of desires existing wholly apart from the shedding of blood." In the tradition of the great hunter-naturalists from John James Audubon before him to Aldo Leopold

Shiras placed one-man deer shacks throughout the camp's property, where hunters stayed for several weeks at a time.

after, Shiras found in deer hunting not only a journey into the heart of nature but a journey that reveals mysteries of the human soul and the behavior of white-tailed deer.

The all-inspiring motive of every deer hunter, Shiras argued, should be fair play in the deer woods and in deer camp. A deer hunter's life must consist of three basic elements: anticipation, realization and reminiscence. Shiras realized the real enjoyment of the deer hunting arises from the freedom it grants us from business cares and social artificiality. He underscores this point in his diary: "We hopefully sit for hours shivering on the limb of a mountain oak and contentedly return to deer camp empty-handed."

Shiras' profound deer hunting creed, developed at the legendary Whitefish Lake Deer Camp, won the immediate approval and appreciation of President Theodore Roosevelt, as it should for all of us.

BUC

EL

Christmas Meat

HUNTING AT THE ELKHORN

Christmas Meat. Watercolor by C.M. Russell, 1915. Courtesy of C.M. Russell Museum

"As we grow older, I think most of us become less keen about that part of the hunt which consists in the killing. I know that as far as I am concerned, I have long gone past the stage when the chief end of a hunting trip is the bag. One or two bucks ... to keep the camp supplied, will furnish all the sport necessary to give zest and point to a trip in the wilderness."

— Theodore Roosevelt,
The Deer Family, 1902

Bang! Bang! Bang! Three reports issued from Theodore Roosevelt's famous Winchester Model 1876 — serial number 38647 — and a magnificent Badlands buck lay dead in its tracks. The buck fell on Buck Hill, west of Medora, N.D., near his legendary Elkhorn Ranch in the heart of the Dakota Badlands.

On that day, Sept. 14, 1884, the 25-year-old dude from New York wore a custom-made buckskin outfit that cost $100, the equivalent of $1,000 or more today. He also carried a Bowie knife and scabbard custom-made by Tiffany & Co., which was tucked into his cartridge belt. There was only one 19th-century Tiffany silver-mounted Bowie knife, and it was made exclusively for TR. According to gun historian R.L. Wilson, the knife had a 7½-inch blade, and the scabbard of sterling silver had an engraving of a buckskin-clad frontiersman on one side and a white-tailed deer on the other. The cartridge belt was secured with the rare Winchester "Bear's Head" closure plate of nickeled brass.

TR described the deluxe Winchester Model 1876 in .45-75 caliber as "the best weapon I ever had." Stocked and sighted to suit him by the Winchester Repeating Arms Co., the rifle sported panel scenes engraved by John Ulrich. The white-tailed buck engraved in the center panel of the left receiver was patterned after a drawing by George Catlin. The rifle contained the earliest scroll work of William E. Stokes done for Winchester. Although TR owned at least three Model 1876s, the .45-75 caliber was his favorite deer rifle and

dominated the gun cabinet at the Elkhorn Ranch between 1884 and 1896. Even so, each of those Winchester 1876s were specially engraved and built at TR's request.

Winchester firearms and ammunition were packaged and sent to TR in crates, sometimes a dozen at a time. They arrived in an official horse-drawn Winchester Wagon with painted logo. TR called these rifles his "beloved Winchesters," his "faithful Winchesters." At one time, he owned 20 Winchester rifles.

In his celebrated book *Hunting Trips of a Ranchman* (1885), which tells of his early deer hunts in the Badlands, TR describes the downing of a magnificent buck with his famous rifle:

"It was some little time after the sun had set, and I was hurrying back to camp, riding down along a winding creek at a gallop. The middle of the bottom was covered with brush, while the steep, grassy, rounded hills on each side sent off spurs into the valley, the part between every two spurs making a deep pocket. The horse's feet were unshod and he made very little noise, coming down against the wind.

"While passing a deep pocket, I heard from within it a snort and stamping feet, the well-known sounds made by a startled deer. Pulling up short I jumped off the horse — it was Manitou — who instantly began feeding with perfect indifference to what he probably regarded as an irrational freak of his master; and, aiming as well as I could

Left, a portrait of young Theodore Roosevelt. Right, Roosevelt with his Winchester Model 1876 rifle.

Opposite page and this page: Theodore Roosevelt Collection. Harvard College Library.

The Adirondack Museum. Blue Mountain Lake, N.Y.

in the gathering dusk, held the rifle well ahead of a shadowy gray object which was scudding along the base of the hill towards the mouth of the pocket. The ball struck in front of and turned the deer, which then started obliquely up the hill. A second shot missed it; and I then ... knelt down and pointed the rifle against the sky line, at the place where the deer seemed likely to top the bluff.

"Immediately afterwards, the buck appeared, making the last jump with a great effort which landed him square on the edge, as sharply outlined as a silhouette against the fading Western light. My rifle bead was just above him; pulling it down I fired, as the buck paused for a second to recover himself from his last great bound, and with a crash the mighty antlered beast came rolling down the hill, the bullet having broke his back behind the shoulders, afterwards going out through his chest."

TR was born in 1858, the year the great deer-slayer Meshach Browning wrote his deer hunting memoirs, *Forty Years the Life of a Hunter*. As a boy, TR often listened to his father read Browning's hair-splitting tales. Those storied jack-lighting hunts by canoe on the waterways of the Allegheny Mountains would soon be re-created by the 15-year-old Roosevelt on Lake St. Regis in the Adirondacks. The first such hunt occurred July 5, 1876, with guides Hank Martin and Mose Sawyer. In his time-honored book *The Wilderness Hunter* (1893), Roosevelt recalls bagging a buck with his .38-caliber Ballard sporting rifle:

"My first attempt at big-game shooting, when a boy, was 'jacking' for deer in the Adirondacks, on a small lake surrounded by the grand Northern forests of birch and beech, pine, spruce and fir. I killed a spike buck; and while I have never been willing to kill another in this manner, I cannot say I regret having once had the experience.

"The ride over the glassy, black water, the witch-craft of such silent progress through the mystery of the night, cannot but impress one. There is pleasure in the mere buoyant gliding of the birch-bark

Jacking Deer. A.F. Tait, circa 1870s. Wash on paper.

canoe, with its curved bow and stern; nothing else that floats possesses such grace, such frail and delicate beauty, as this true craft of the wilderness, which is as much a creature of the wild woods as the deer themselves.

"The light streaming from the bark lantern in the bow cuts a glaring lane through the gloom; in it all objects stand out like magic, shining for a moment white and ghastly and then vanishing into the impenetrable darkness; while all the time the paddler in the stern makes not so much as a ripple, and there is never a sound but the occasional splash of a muskrat, or the moaning uloo-oo — uloo-uloo of an owl from the deep forest; and at last perchance the excitement of a shot at a buck, standing at gaze, with luminous eye balls."

Like his friend George Shiras III, TR denounced this hunting tactic well before the New York state Legislature outlawed the practice of jacking and killing deer in water in 1897. In 1877, he shot his second white-tailed buck in the Adirondacks for his

Zoological Collection at Harvard with his hand-engraved Lefaucheux Pinfire, a 12-gauge, breech-loading shotgun he received for Christmas in 1876.

Ever since boyhood, Roosevelt dreamed of living out the deer hunting tales of James Fenimore Cooper's Natty Bumppo, and emulating the life and adventures of John James Audubon. He called Cooper's hero, Natty Bumppo, "one of the undying men of story," a phrase that applies well to TR himself.

In his *Autobiography* (1913), TR acknowledges that "the first two or three bucks I ever saw gave me buck fever badly." He quickly overcame this malady and began fulfilling his boyhood dreams in the late 1870s. He wished to re-create the life of the early American deerslayers as he "outgeneraled" deer on foot, snowshoes and in canoes, and killed

The verandah of the Elkhorn ranch house, photographed by Teddy Roosevelt, 1885. Leaning against the elk rack at center is TR's Model 1876 .45-75 rifle. At top right are his engraved Colt six-shooters in a hand-tooled holster.

Theodore Roosevelt Collection. Harvard College Library.

The Elkhorn ranch house.

Theodore Roosevelt Collection. Harvard College Library.

them with his Sharps "Old Reliable" Mid-Range Borchardt 40-2⅝ in Maine's northern woods.

On Sept. 7, 1878, he traveled to Lake Mattawamkeag in Maine's Aroostock County, which lies northeast of Silver Ridge, where Fred Goodwin would later assemble one of the world's greatest white-tailed deer antler collections. On Lake Mattawamkeag, TR eventually built a deer camp that stayed in the family name for almost a century. A plaque at "Bible Point" on the lakeshore marks where TR went to sit, reflect, read the Bible and hunt white-tailed deer.

From this September 1878 deer hunt came one of TR's favorite deer camp stories. On Sept. 16, as he still-hunted the banks of Lake Mattawamkeag with his lifelong guide Bill Sewall, they spotted a buck with a dark, palmated and heavy-tined rack.

"Shoot!" Sewall whispered, and the young Roosevelt eased off the Sharps "Old Reliable" Mid-Range Borchardt. The buck dropped in its tracks.

"You've got him!" cried Sewall as he ran to examine the downed animal.

"How did you do it?" Sewall asked.

"I aimed for the crease behind the front shoulder, held low in the area of the sixth rib," young Roosevelt announced with certainty.

"You done real well," Sewall hollered at the Harvard student. "Real well! You hit the buck in the eye!"

In March 1879, TR returned to Aroostock County, Maine, for another deer hunt with his guides Wilmot Dow and Bill Sewall, known as "the track-hound on the deer trail."

I shot a buck, he wrote to his sister Anna Roosevelt Cowles, "a coon and some rabbits and partridges and trapped a lynx and a fox — so my trip was a success in every way."

In August 1884, he bought a ranch on the Little Missouri River in the Dakota Badlands 30 miles north of Medora and just south of Whitetail Creek. He called it the Elkhorn Ranch, after finding

a massive set of interlocked elk antlers on the site where he intended to build a camp. Initially, the Elkhorn Ranch consisted of only a small deer shack called "The Den," where TR and his two Maine guides hung out.

In August and September 1884, the buckskin-clad Roosevelt went on a seven-week deer hunting expe-dition to Wyoming's Bighorn Mountains. All of his Winchester equipment, 1,700 rounds of ammuni-tion, and a complete wardrobe of deerskin hunting attire was loaded into a covered wagon. A mountain man named Norman Lebo, a Civil War veteran, and TR's guide and Elkhorn cowboy, William Merrifield, accompanied Roosevelt.

Saved: A Hard Chase. A.F. Tait, 1874. Oil on canvas.

Adirondack Museum. Blue Mountain Lake, N.Y.

On Aug. 29, 1884, TR rode Old Manitou, frequently called "the best deer hunting horse in the Badlands," along the side of a steep ridge in an attempt to avoid silhouetting himself against the blue sky. Suddenly, Manitou slipped on loose rocks and fell backward. Roosevelt leaped from the saddle

and avoided being crushed against the rocks. After two somersaults, the sorrel stallion, TR's beloved and respected companion, recovered, and both continued the hunt.

Several hours later, Roosevelt spotted three black-tailed bucks grazing in a small clearing. After easing from the saddle, he fired his Winchester Model 1876. The bullet struck the ground in front of them, causing them to bound off unharmed. Moments later, two of the bucks reappeared abreast of each other. TR squeezed off another shot, bringing down both bucks with one shot. In his diary, he termed it "the best shot" of his life. He paced off the distance at 400 yards. He took seven shots to kill seven more deer on this trip.

As he chased deer through the Bighorns' deep gorges, he recalled his earlier deer hunts in the Adirondacks and northern Maine. On Sept. 17, 1884, with their pack ponies laden with hides and horns, the men broke camp and started for the Elkhorn. A correspondent for the *St. Paul Pioneer Press* characterized TR after his return as "healthy, strong, rugged, bronzed and in the prime of health," taking on the image of his friend Owen Wister's "The Virginian."

By Spring 1885, the Elkhorn cabin, which was made from cottonwood logs, was nearly complete. It contained eight large rooms, two fireplaces, a huge porch and 7-foot beamed ceilings. The walls of this 30-by-60-foot hewed structure contained deerskins, antlers, bookshelves for his world-class hunting library, and miscellaneous deer hunting memorabilia. The memorabilia included everything from deer prints to classic Winchester deer rifles resting across elk antlers.

In *Hunting Trips of a Ranchman*, Roosevelt wrote, "From the deer horns ranged along the walls and thrust into the beams and rafters hang heavy overcoats of wolf-skin or coon-skin and otter-fur and beaver-fur caps and gauntlets."

Roosevelt believed no ranch man who loves sport could be without Van Dyke's *The Still-Hunter* and John Dean Caton's

The Antelope and Deer of America. He kept both original editions of these deer books at the Elkhorn, and both were signed by their authors, with whom Roosevelt corresponded. TR's big-game library now reposes as a special collection in the Library of Congress. According to Frederick R. Goff, former chief of the rare book division, Caton's *The Antelope and Deer of America* formed the cornerstone of Roosevelt's hunting library. His mother gave him the autographed copy as a Christmas gift in 1877 when he was 19 years old.

Roosevelt spent his time at the Elkhorn reading books and periodicals, writing his hunting trilogy, listening to the wind in the cottonwoods, hunting deer in the hills near the ranch, and enjoying the sweet taste of white-tailed venison in the evenings in front of the fireplace. Occasionally, he left the rocking chair in his study, stepped out onto the verandah with his Winchester Model 1876, and shot a whitetail grazing in front of the cabin.

After field dressing the animal, TR returned to his favorite deer hunting poems, such as Ernest McGaffey's "The Twelve-Tined Buck."

But over the pines and cedars
Re-echoed a distant horn,
And a hound's faint bay chimed with it
In the hush of the waking morn.

And then from a balsam thicket
Came the sound of a sudden crash,
And a twelve-tined buck sprang out and stood
By the side of a quaking ash.

His horns were brown as the Autumn,
And his hoofs like jasper shone,
And his dark eyes gleamed in the dawning
As he snuffed the breeze alone.

And then as the gathering echoes
Brought up the hounds' deep cry,
He passed like a steel-gray shadow
And scattered the pine-cones dry.

And down through the tall pine timber,
As an arrow will cut its way,
He fled to the quickening clamor
Of the hounds with their mellow bay.

"Here at the Elkhorn," he told people, "the romance of my life began." Indeed, at this deer camp, TR played out the life of early-American deerslayers with the zest, high spirits and emotional enthusiasm

A stereoscopic photo card of a Badlands deer hunting camp near the Elkhorn, circa 1887. Notice the deerskin jacket, snowshoes, skis, hatchets and well-worn Winchester rifles.

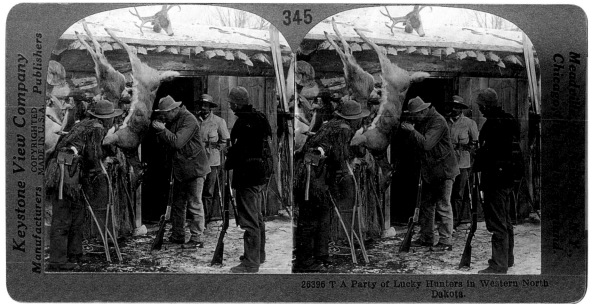

Rob Wegner Photo Collection.

A deer hunting postcard from TR's day, circa 1900. Two Black Hills hunters bring in three bucks.

of Meshach Browning, John James Audubon, Henry William Herbert "Frank Forester," William Elliott, Philip Tome, Oliver Hazard Perry and all the rest of our great, cultural deer-hunting heroes.

In the mid-1880s and early 1890s, TR had the time and energy to roam Western game lands in pursuit of deer. For weeks on end he glorified in the adventure and excitement of deer hunting while absorbing the mood and spirit of coursing deer with his hounds, hunting horns and Manitou. Like Audubon and Frank Forester before him, this was "the most exciting form of deer hunting imaginable." It appealed to his sense of adventure, romance and challenge. TR characterized it this way in *The Wilderness Hunter*:

"The coursing on the prairie, especially after deer, is an exceedingly manly and attractive sport; the furious galloping, often over rough ground with an occasional deep washout or gully, the sight of the gallant hounds running and tackling, and the exhilaration of the pure air and wild surroundings, all combine to give it a peculiar zest. ... Of all sports possible in civilized countries, riding to hounds is perhaps the best if followed as it should be, for the sake of the strong excitement, with as much simplicity as possible, and not merely as a fashionable amusement. It tends to develop moral no less than physical qualities; the rider needs nerve and head; he must possess daring and resolution, as well as a good deal of bodily skill and a certain amount of wiry toughness and endurance."

While riding Manitou and following his cherished, wire-haired deer hounds Rob and Brandy, TR sported a pair of silver-mounted California spurs marked "H. Messing & Son Makers/San Jose, Cal." and engraved with the TR monogram. With his buckskin shirt and trousers, which were custom-tai-

Amon Carter Museum. Fort Worth, Texas.

lored by the Widow Maddox, seamstress of the Badlands, plus his alligator boots, sealskin chaps, tooled saddle and silver-mounted Bowie knife, TR had the look of a dandy cowboy deerslayer. In a letter to his sister Anna Roosevelt Cowles, dated Aug. 17, 1884, TR commented on his attire:

"I wear a sombrero, silk-neckerchief, fringed buckskin shirt, sealskin chaparajos or riding-trousers and alligator-hide boots and with my pearl-hilted revolver and beautifully furnished Winchester rifle, I feel able to face anything."

In 1886, Roosevelt continued to enjoy his deer hunting life at the Elkhorn with books, guns, horses, hounds and deer. He had already acquired one of the finest libraries on big-game hunting in North America. At the end of his daily Badlands deer hunts, he sat in his large rocking chair in front of the blazing fireplace and read *Poems of the Rod and Gun* (1886) by Isaac McLellan (1806-1899). To the attention and delight of his lifelong deer hunting guides from Maine, Bill Sewall and Will Dow, he quoted from McLellan's poem "Deer-Hunting in Maine":

Far in the South, the stout cavalier
On galloping courser rides down the deer,
Far soundeth his hulloo and bugle horn
From the broad plantation, at break of morn;
Thro' bush and tho' brier, thro' tangled glade,
Like a charging troop sweeps the cavalcade,
And many a noble buck of ten-tines
Is brought to bay ere the day declines.

In Fall 1886, the young cowboy/deer hunter read

The Cowboy by Frederic Remington, Oil on canvas, 1902, eventually graced the cover of Roosevelt's book *Ranch Life and the Hunting Trail*.

several newspaper articles in the *Dickinson Press* and *Bismarck Tribune* about a world-class 22-point whitetail shot by Olaf Anderson. This hunter was coursing deer with hounds at Fort Stevenson, a short distance northeast of the Elkhorn Ranch. TR not only dreamed of bucks like this one, but pursued them for two reasons: To acquire magnificent trophies for his world-famous antler collection at Sagamore Hill, a national historic site, and to procure venison for the cowpunchers' pot at the Elkhorn.

Roosevelt followed the story of the Anderson buck with great interest. This buck, with its nontypical score of $232\frac{1}{8}$ points, would become the earliest nontypical white-tailed buck to enter the record book kept by the Boone and Crockett Club, which Roosevelt founded in December 1887. This buck still reigns as the No. 2 nontypical whitetail of North Dakota. Its original mount is now part of Larry Huffman's "Legendary Whitetails Collection."

"Symmetry is the deer's calling card," says white-tailed deer enthusiast Gordon Whittington. "Each antler has 11 points, each beam is $24\frac{5}{8}$ inches, and even the drop tines match in length and shape."

TR considered it the finest white-tailed buck of its time. He would have loved to have known that Anderson trained his horse to stop in its tracks when it heard him click back the hammer on his old Winchester Model 1866 carbine.

Roosevelt also considered a buck killed by his nearest neighbor, Howard Eaton, to be one of the finest whitetails of the time. This 32-pointer, shot in

Theodore Roosevelt loved to hunt deer on horseback, as seen in this 1902 Mississippi hunt.

South Dakota in 1870, remains that state's No. 2 nontypical with a Boone and Crockett score of 250⁶/₈. Its mount hung for years above the fireplace at the Eaton Ranch, which lies just north of the Elkhorn where Big Beaver Creek meets the Little Missouri River.

Early in November 1887, Roosevelt began a five-week deer hunt at the Elkhorn with his new deluxe .45-90 Winchester Model 1886. He had received it from the factory Sept. 30, 1887. He used this rifle regularly on deer hunts from 1887 to 1894 in the river bottoms of the Little Missouri. On these hunts, TR often put his purebred Scotch stag-hounds, Rob and Brandy, in the dense cottonwoods along the river, with a horseman to guide them and rout out deer. Meanwhile, TR and his cowpunchers, with Winchesters in hand, rode point to point outside the cottonwoods to shoot fleeing deer. All venison from this hunt went toward the winter's meat supply. In *Outdoor Pastimes of an American Hunter* (1905), Roosevelt estimated the annual take of whitetails for

the ranch's meat consumption during the mid-1880s at 40 deer.

Reviewers of Roosevelt's work characterized these highly charged hunts as "tinglingly alive, masculine and vascular," as the next three examples illustrate. The dramatic excitement of Frederic Remington's drawings and oil paintings — and those of Charlie Russell, A.B. Frost and Henry Sandham — add flare and vigor to TR's deer-hunting stories. His prose is so immediate you can smell the smoking venison, experience the sleepy rest on bearskins, and hear the roaring fire, old Brandy's clamorous yelling, and the icy wind moaning in the cottonwoods.

While following Rob and Brandy one day on a November 1887 hunt, TR shot a white-tailed buck in the bottoms below the ranch house.

"The river was low, and my post was at its edge, with in front of me the broad sandy flat sparsely covered with willow-brush. Deer are not much afraid of an ordinary noisy hound; they will play round in front of him, head and flag in air; but with Rob it was different. The gray, wolfish beast, swift and silent, threw them into a panic of terror, and in headlong flight they would seek safety from him in the densest thicket.

"On the evening in question, one of my cowboys went into the brush with the hounds. I had hardly ridden to my place and dismounted when I heard old Brandy give tongue, the bluffs echoing back his long-drawn baying. Immediately afterward a young buck appeared, coming along the sandy river-bed, trotting or cantering; and very handsome he looked, stepping with a light, high action, his glossy coat glistening, his head thrown back, his white flag flaunting. My bullet struck him too far back, and he went on, turning into the woods. Then the dogs appeared, old Brandy running the scent, while the eager gaze-hound made wide half-circles around him as he ran; while the cowboy, riding a vicious yellow mustang, galloped behind, cheering them on. As they struck the bloody trail, they broke into clamorous yelling, and tore at full speed into the woods. A minute or two later the sound ceased, and I knew they had run into the quarry."

On one of the last days he hunted in November 1887, TR shot two black-tailed deer, a doe and a buck, with one bullet. He encountered them feeding on the side of a steep hill. After a careful stalk, he got within 50 yards of them.

"Peering over the brink of the cliff-like slope up which I had clambered, I saw them standing in such a position that the neck of the doe covered the buck's shoulder. The chance was too tempting to be lost. My bullet broke the doe's neck and, of course, she fell where she was; but the buck went off, my next two or three shots missing him. However, we followed his bloody trail through the high pass he had crossed, down a steep slope, and roused him from the brushwood in a valley bottom. He soon halted and lay down again, making off at a faltering gallop when approached, and the third time we came up to him he was too weak to rise. He had splendid antlers."

During the next few years, TR's political life as New York's civil service commissioner began to impinge on his deer hunts. In Fall 1888, however, he hunted deer in the Kootenai country of British Columbia. He shot a deer and enjoyed eating its venison in front of a fire at a camp on Kootenai Lake with William Merrifield, his deer hunting companion and Elkhorn cowboy.

In 1890, TR again shot numerous deer in the Badlands near the Elkhorn as he rode in the saddle morning till night. He sometimes covered more than 100 miles in a day. Nights around the campfire were always filled with romance, reading and storytelling. The mainstay of each evening meal was venison — fried, broiled or roasted — with an occasional interlude of ducks or prairie chickens served with TR's favorite wild plum and buffalo berry jellies and jams, made by the ranch foreman's wife.

On the last day of his 1894 deer hunt at the Elkhorn — and with the last bullet he fired from his Winchester Model 1886 — he killed a magnificent 10-point whitetail. It was to be the last of his Badlands bucks.

"By good luck, the buck, evidently flurried, came right on the edge of the woods next to me, and as he passed, running like a quarter-horse, I held well ahead of him and pulled the trigger. The bullet broke his neck and down he went — a fine fellow with a handsome ten-point head, and fat as a prize sheep for it was just before the rut. Then we rode home, and I sat in a rocking-chair on the ranch house verandah, looking across the wide, sandy river bed at the strangely shaped buttes and the groves of shimmering cottonwoods until the sun went down and the frosty air bade me go in."

During TR's time, deer hunting was not only acceptable, it was considered a commendable form of recreation. Fortunately, most Americans still find it acceptable, when done for meat consumption. By the standards of his day, TR's attitudes toward deer and deer hunting were enlightened. His bags were modest and selective. He enjoyed pursuing whitetails in the wilderness the same way he did everything: with vigor, exuberance

Roosevelt's nearest neighbor, Howard Eaton, shot this 32-pointer in 1870. It scored 250⅝ Boone and Crockett points, and was TR's favorite buck and the world's largest nontypical whitetail at the time.

Courtesy of Jack Brittingham.

Rob Wegner Photo Collection.

and emotional intensity.

His deer hunting narratives display that same energy. He was, after all, a romantic who saw the glory, glamour and high adventure of chasing deer in the wilderness. And he certainly did not, as hunting historian Paul Schullery argues, "deny himself the gratification of enthusiastic literary celebration." He portrayed the deer camp experience as "the wine of life." And he drank that wine with brandy. His colorful prose about these deer hunts remains unsurpassed, and will lurk in the collective unconsciousness of deer hunters for time immemorial.

"Where the whitetail can be followed with horse and hound," he writes in *The Deer Family* (1902), "the sport is, of course, of the very highest order. To be able to ride through woods and over rough country at full speed, rifle or shotgun in hand, and then to leap off and shoot at a running object, is to show that one has the qualities which made the cavalry of Forrest so formidable in the Civil War. There could be no better training for the mounted rifleman, the most efficient type of modern soldier."

For Theodore Roosevelt, deer hunting was intimately attached to an intense devotion to manliness: Deer hunting was synonymous with training for war, as well as finding one's place and peace within the natural world. TR found his place and peace with nature while buck hunting at the Elkhorn.

After returning to the civilized racket of New York City, TR dreamed of big bucks and the welcoming flicker of firelight in the Elkhorn's windows. Such scenes are romantically portrayed in Charlie Russell's watercolor "Christmas Meat," 1915, as seen in the opening pages of this chapter.

On Sept. 14, 1901, the day President McKinley died, Vice President Roosevelt was hunting whitetails in the Adirondacks. On Sept. 23, 1901, the 42-year-old TR became the 26th president of the United States, the youngest president in American history. America had one of its greatest deerslayers in the Oval Office managing the country's affairs — buck hunter incarnate, TR of the Elkhorn.

Now, or Never. Oil on canvas. Philip R. Goodwin.

LIFE AT THE LUND
ESTEAD

Courtesy of Fred P. "Wigs" Lund.

"For supper the opening day, we always had fresh heart, liver, bacon, fried onions, and lot of it. No one would admit to not liking this bill of fare because it would have been almost sacrilegious to serve anything else in a legitimate hunting camp the opening day of the season. I'm sure that most of the greenhorns ate it for fear of being drummed out of camp."

— Fred P. "Wigs" Lund.
I Mind: Memories of the
Old Hunting Camp Days, 1969

In the early 1880s, Hakon O. Lund (1866-1943) — one of America's first and most colorful conservation wardens — hunted whitetails at a unique deer camp called "The Homestead." The camp, located near Camp Two Lake and Trout Lake in Wisconsin's Bayfield County, sat nine miles south of a small town called Iron River. This town was founded because John A. Pettingill — known as the founding father of Iron River — decided to hunt deer there. Pettingill is remembered for downing one of Wisconsin's heaviest deer: a 10-pointer with an estimated live weight of 477 pounds. The buck fell in 1906 south of Iron River near The Homestead.

Iron River was a bawdy town. When the government allocated property for homesteading this timberland of huge white and Norway pines, the town's population exploded to 3,500. To accommodate the 4,000 lumberjacks in 30 lumber camps within 10 miles of Iron River, the town built 37 saloons. The editor of the *Iron River Homestead* reported, "Iron River had more drunks per square foot than any other town in the United States."

In his stories of northern Wisconsin, *And That's The Way It Was* (1973), Fred P. "Wigs" Lund, Hakon's son, noted when old-timers finished a story about Iron River's early days, they often said: "Yup, she was quite a town. The common saying was Iron River, Hurley, and Hell, and makin' Iron River the best of the three wasn't much of a compliment, because she was a rip-snorter worse than the cesspools of Hell."

During the 1880s, venison was the common meat of logging camps and meat markets. It cost 8 cents per pound in Wisconsin, and deer season opened in mid-August and closed Nov. 30. No restrictions were placed on the sex, size or number of deer that could be taken on one license. A combination of uncontrolled forest fires, and market and subsistence hunting caused dramatic declines in the herd.

On Jan. 20, 1885, the *Wisconsin State Journal* reported that during the 1884 deer season, one Bayfield County hunter shot 75 deer, five moose and one bear. Before the 1880s ended, Hakon Lund and his Homestead boys experienced many restrictions: shining deer, hunting deer with dogs and selling venison were all prohibited by law, and the deer season lasted 31 days.

The deer herd still sunk to an all-time low around 1910. The bag eventually was cut to 10 in 1917.

A deer-hunting postcard from 1912.

Rob Wegner Photo Collection.

The Homestead deer camp consisted of a two-story log cabin that measured 16 feet by 24 feet. It had, as "Wigs" Lund reported in his camp memoirs, *I Mind* (1969), "a shanty kitchen tacked on and a front porch that tilted towards 'Medicine Bow.'"

Like most deer hunters, H.O. Lund loved to hang around deer shacks and old cabins in the back country. And like most of his crew, he used a Winchester .30-30 Model 1894, which had buckhorn sights and an octagonal barrel. It weighed 9 pounds and held 10 shells.

"I don't know how many deer he killed with that Winchester rifle, but he didn't miss many," Wigs wrote. "My father's motto was one man, one rifle, one shell, one shot, one deer."

Old man Lund never shaved during deer season. His old black-felt, broad-brimmed hat and lumberjack trousers made of a heavy grayish-black material made him look like an "old shacker" who hadn't left the deer woods for more than 20 years. Wigs wrote a chapter on Hakon's old deer hunting pants in *I Mind*:

"As the years passed, the many seasons of deer hunting took their toll. The brush and briars shredded the bottoms and tore through the knees. Every night during the season my dad had to mend those trousers. He darned them until there was nothing to attach the yarn to and then he patched. Eventually, there were patches over patches and as each piece of cloth was sewn on, the trousers took on weight. I'm sure they must have weighed nine to ten pounds dry. As I look at his picture taken during the last fall he hunted and shot a buck, the only part of the original trousers are from the waist band down to the middle of his upper leg. He always looked for strong, serviceable cloth for patching, so every piece was a different color. The buttons in the front had been replaced many times and after the suspender buttons had pulled out so many times that there was no place left to sew another one on, he used a six penny nail and it worked damn well. They were permanently bent at the knees and when he hung them up at night they looked as if they were in a half-crouching position and ready to jump."

Rob Wegner Photo Collection.

This world-class buck hung in J. Widmer Smith's Standard Service Station in Loretta, Wis., in the 1940s. Although the buck was never scored, it remains a star attraction at the J. Widmer Smith Antler Collection in Hayward, Wis.

At The Homestead camp, 12 to 18 men gathered each year in a tightly knit social bond to hunt deer. One morning, while feeding buckwheat pancakes to this crew — commonly called "The Ridge Runners Company" — Lund announced to the nimrods, "Feeding you fellows is just like throwing wood shavings into Hell."

The Homestead consisted of 160 acres, with the nearest deer camp miles away. As with most legendary deer camps, colorful landmarks became special places on The Homestead's "sacred" property: Pole Road, The White Way, Camp 2 Forks, Happle's Crossing, Hessey's Landing, Miller's Pothole and the Big Ravine. Each place had its own intriguing story among the locals to explain its unique name.

These places ingrained themselves in the minds of Wigs Lund and other camp members. When watching 20 red-clad deer hunters hiking up a hill to start a deer drive, Lund reflected on the day ahead:

"The sun would make their coats so brilliant against the snow that was so white and sparkly. It was a warm feeling to see the smoke rising straight out of the chimney at noon, and to catch the first glimpse of the lamps in the windows as it was getting dark. Another wonderful meal would be waiting, with a pleasant evening ahead listening to stories of the day and of hunting incidents forty years before. This was a part of my life from childhood to adult age."

When deer season drew to a close and hunters began to leave The Homestead, Wigs Lund always felt pangs of loneliness. Thoughts of breaking camp just made matters worse. On the last day of many deer seasons, he stood on a hillside and watched the sun go down:

"To me the quietness, the beauty of the pines against the snow, and that immensely big expanse of country was something I could never seem to get enough of."

Their rustic, rickety cabin with its "Round Oak" heater stood in a large valley with one open end. The Lunds called the outhouse in the woods to the north "The Cabin in the Pines." The water pump, located in the lower part of the valley, produced cold, clear water from 98 feet below. It took 98 strokes of the pump handle to bring it to the surface. According to H.O. Lund, "the filling of two 14-quart galvanized pails was a good meal settler."

The rules of The Homestead were unwritten and never questioned: no booze, no rough language, no loaded guns in camp, no gambling and no all-night card games. Lund believed no respectable deer camp should operate without a spittoon or nightly game of smear. Even so, the highlight of each evening, which often entailed a good deal of table pounding, determined who would get the big buck on The Big Drive in the morning.

The deer drives by Lund and his hunters proved successful each year because old man Lund scheduled and carefully planned them well before the

evening smear game started.

"If General Ludendorf had planned his big drive against the Allies in World War I as carefully as H.O. Lund laid his plans for our big drive, he might have won the war," Wigs wrote.

Old man Lund planned the same drives year after year: The Camp 20 Drive, The Little Trout Lake Drive, The White Way Drive and The Rye Patch Drive were among the favorites. With fresh snow and the wind in the right direction, his crew of

Rob Wegner Photo Collection.

about 15 to 16 guns awaited their orders. The old man's instructions to the greenhorns were explicit:

"Keep the wind in your right ear. Walk slowly and keep your eyes peeled. There are bucks in these woods with horns the size of rockin' chairs!"

Lund insisted the drive be slow, methodical and quiet. He had it all figured out.

"Why bang away at a spooked deer, hightailing it like the hammers of hell for the next county, when you could connect with one that was loping along?"

Deer hunting camp at an old homestead in northwestern Wisconsin near Iron River, 1920.

The windup of Lund's deer drives took only about 10 minutes. With the final landmarks coming into view, the drivers knew all hell would soon break loose. Wigs Lund saw it many times:

"The rifles of the men posted would open up from all sides, and the cannonading would sound like the siege of Vicksburg. We connected and hung up many's the buck on The Big Drive."

The results of this drive frequently appeared in Iron River newspapers. According to one newspaper account, young P.O. Lund finally shot his first deer after 30 days of deer driving and 200 rounds of ammunition. This item, however, should not denigrate the shooting abilities of the many 21 carat "buck hunters of the first water" that hung out at The Homestead.

The Homestead regulars represented a cross section of American society. Some were local residents, some were "downstaters" from Milwaukee and Madison, and some were out-of-state hunters from Minneapolis and St. Paul, Minn. Everyone fit in and seemed congenial; everyone was awakened in the morning by the infernal rapping of Lund's knife on the stovepipe.

"The rapping on the stovepipe and the smell of fried side pork could rouse a dead man," wrote Wigs Lund in his deer-camp memoirs.

Who else were regulars at The Homestead? In the inner circle was rich Uncle Miller, who smoked Turkish cigarettes and frequently showed up in his Packard touring car. This greenhorn from the big city soon became aware of The Homestead's rules and regulations.

Everyone in camp looked forward to the arrival of

Homer Pearson and his wife, below, pose with Homer's 31-pointer, which weighed 217 pounds field dressed.

Rob Wegner Photo Collection

Rob Wegner Photo Collection.

Homer Pearson and his wife, above, arrive back at the Pearson homestead. His buck eventually scored 233⁷⁄₈ Boone and Crockett points. A postcard of the full-body mount, right, of Homer Pearson's buck, shot in 1937.

Giles Meisenheimer, an airplane pilot who always threatened to fly to camp some year and land on the 11-acre field behind the cabin called "The Rye Patch." But he never did. Meisenheimer usually arrived with enough gear and rifles to equip a squad of Marines. Wigs Lund claimed Meisenheimer usually "came out to our hunting camp with more equipment than Lewis and Clark took with them when they explored the Louisiana Purchase."

Meisenheimer always tried to keep his feet dry by applying at least a dozen different kinds of boot oil and grease to his leather boots. He figured the more the better. The entire Homestead eventually smelled like a mixture of sweet fern, boot grease and wet leather.

P.J. Savage, or "Uncle Pete," was "chief cook of the booya." He provided The Homestead with an amazing repertoire of deer camp tales that were masterpieces of imagination and exaggeration. His size and

Rob Wegner Photo Collection.

stirring gestures demanded the attention of all present. One night, Uncle Pete remarked that "something should be done to those beans to take the firecrackers out of them!" He directed his remark to a greenhorn named "Willie" who promptly mashed his delicious baked beans into a thick, pasty mush.

Savage, the long-time editor of the *Iron River Pioneer*, gave The Homestead excellent coverage in his newspaper, including the trying times of such deer camp regulars as Dr. Fred "Cedar-foot" Johnson Sr., Bige Buchanan and Brad Besemann, a deputy warden whose bouts with John Barleycorn were well known. However, Besemann never lapsed from the perpendicular nor took a drink while at The Homestead.

Besemann often graced the pages of the local newspaper, as did the shooting exploits of Phil Lund, who, as Wigs observed, "shot up more ammunition than had been used in the Spanish-American War."

One also thinks of another camp regular in the

Above, a nightly game of cards. Notice the wallpaper along the ceiling and beams. Left, Wigs Lund with a young member of the Lund family, his deer-hunting knife and his Winchester Model 1895 sporting rifle.

"Whitetail Expedition." This was "General" (Six Star) C.A. "Pete" Peterson, who shot many bucks with his old Winchester .32 Special, as reported in the *Iron River Pioneer*. In addition, Peterson loved to eat venison tenderloins while in camp. Wigs Lund characterized him as a "true-blue, 100 percent, 21-carat buckhunter of the first water ... who had the energy of a diesel motor, the spirit of an

Fred P. "Wigs" Lund.

Fred P. "Wigs" Lund.

Arabian stallion and the stamina that would put Eric the Red to shame."

Area game wardens also visited The Homestead to compare notes with Hakon Lund's observations on local deer poachers. These stories of investigations and pursuits of poachers also appeared in the local newspaper.

There were more important matters at The Homestead, however, than making the local news. As with many other deer camps before and after, The Homestead played a significant role in the rites of passage of boys like Phil and Wigs Lund into manhood. Both boys aspired to be one of The Homestead's regulars. Wigs Lund's ascension into the ranks of "the great buckhunters" came at age 14, when H.O. asked him to be a stander on the Camp 20 Drive during the 1926 season. As the drive neared its climax, the boy killed an 8-pointer. In an essay titled "Me, The Mighty Buckhunter," Wigs describes his initiation:

"I was extremely proud when my Uncle Pete congratulated me as if I were a man. Dad now talked to me on a man-to-man basis instead of as a father to

Rob Wegner Photo Collection.

his youngest son. I felt that I was growing up fast!"

In 1937, the 26-year-old Wigs returned to The Homestead for a three-day buck season with the Ridge Runners. Despite a heavy snowfall, the 1937 deer season proved memorable.

In fact, in a larger sense, 1937 remains a significant year in the history of Wisconsin deer hunting. That year, Aldo Leopold, chairman of the newly founded Department of Wildlife Management at the University of Wisconsin in Madison, warned of an impending deer-herd eruption in northern Wisconsin. Leopold's friend Gordon MacQuarrie, who had just become outdoors editor of the *Milwaukee Journal*, echoed Leopold's concerns of an exploding deer herd.

That year, the Wisconsin Conservation Department conducted deer drives throughout the state and estimated the herd at 28.6 deer per section. Why so large? Between 1924 and 1935, the state closed the deer season in odd-numbered years and held buck-only seasons in even-numbered years. In 1937, the Conservation Commission recommended the start of more liberal harvests. As a result, the 1937 Wisconsin deer hunt marked the return of consecutive deer hunting seasons.

That season spurred the first "Save the Deer" clubs and inspired public criticism of the state's deer-management policies. The 1937 season ran Nov. 26-28, and included a bag limit of one forked-horn buck. The license cost $1. Records indicate 90,906 hunters participated in the hunt, resulting in an estimated kill of 14,835 whitetails for a 16 percent success rate. At the end of the 1930s, historian Otis Bersing reported in *A Century of Wisconsin Deer*, "more than two times as many bucks were taken (that year) as were bagged during any deer season of the 1920s."

Homestead regular "Sag" Savage reported in the *Iron River Pioneer* that the 1937 Homestead meat-pole hung heavy with big North Woods bucks. In my conversations with the late Wigs Lund, I learned The Homestead's regulars in '37 bagged 11 antlered

John A. Pettingill's deer camp located south of Iron River, Wis. Pettingill poses with his Winchester Model 1866 carbine, 1906.

bucks in the Big Drives.

Even so, the main deer talk at The Homestead that year revolved around Homer Pearson, a Burnett County farmer who bagged a 31-pointer near The Homestead with his Winchester .30-30 carbine. This buck would eventually score 233$\frac{7}{8}$ nontypical points on the Boone and Crockett scoring system. Members of The Homestead deer camp soon drove to the Friendly Buckhorn Tavern in Rice Lake, Wis., to view the buck's full-body mount. The buck was displayed there for many years, and is now part of Larry Huffman's Legendary Whitetails Collection.

The Homestead, like all other deer camps, had a social beginning and a social ending. The end came in the early 1940s, after more than 50 years of camp memories. Many of the old-timers died, moved away or grew unable to make the trip to camp because of declining health or other social reasons. The group's nucleus gradually disintegrated as the next generation went off to war and to locations across the country to pursue careers.

The cabin's shaky foundation began to rot, causing the floor to bulge. The meatpole sagged and the poker chips molded away, but one could still smell, through the musty odor of decay, Meisenheimer's boot grease. As the wind howled down the chimney, The Homestead began to disappear, and with it went the well and the two-holer in the pines. The site eventually became part of the Chequamegon National Forest.

On their final visit to The Homestead, shortly

A typical scene at a meatpole in northwestern Wisconsin during the early 1930s.

Rob Wegner Photo Collection.

before Hakon's death, old man Lund and Wigs gazed down the valley. The cabin stood as a lonesome structure against the snow — gray, weather-beaten and forlorn. Neither man said anything for a while as memories came to mind. Finally, H.O. cleared his throat and said in a barely audible nostalgic tone: "It sure would be nice to look down there and see the lamps burning in the windows and smoke coming out of the chimney. Those were good days, boy."

In fighting back the tears, Wigs could only say,

Minnesota Historical Society.

"Yah, they sure were."

After his father died in 1943, nostalgia drove Wigs Lund back time and again to the building site. He just wanted to walk down the old road that led to The Homestead one more time. He knew the past was gone, but he would come back again and again, if for no other reason than to stare at the old rusty pails and decayed timbers.

Wigs wrote in his deer hunting journal: "I'm going back next fall and, God willing, I'll go back

Hunters hauling moose and deer out of the timber about 1900. Note the lineup of Winchester rifles resting against the sleigh.

again and again, because somewhere in that enticingly beautiful country that brings back countless memories, there's a big buck. He has hoofprints as large as a small steer and a rack of horns the size of a rockin' chair. He's pokin' around those hills and potholes, and he knows he's got my name on him. If I keep my eye peeled, I'll nail him."

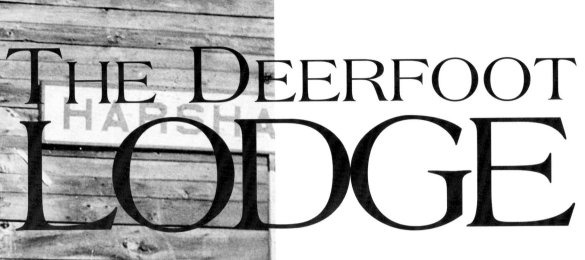

THE DEERFOOT LODGE

"**Once more** 'the frost is on the pumpkin and the fodder is in the shock,' and it is high time we began to think of Lake Laura, the prize buck, and kindred subjects of real importance."

— "Caesar" Rosenberry,
unpublished letter to
members of Deerfoot Lodge,
Oct. 20, 1915.

State Historical Society of Wisconsin.

In Winter 1910, a group of Wisconsin deer hunters from Wausau purchased a 600-acre tract on the shores of Lake Laura in Vilas County in an attempt to enjoy excellent deer hunting for years to come. The purchase included several vacated dwellings of an old Milwaukee timber firm called Land, Log and Timber Co. These buildings included a barn, sleeping shanty, cook shanty and dining room. The property also included the Snake House, a former saloon where drunks went when "over served."

In March 1910, the hunters formed a corporation and filed the articles of incorporation with the secretary of state. Deerfoot Lodge was, apparently, the first Wisconsin corporation ever chartered to hunt deer.

The story of Deerfoot Lodge, however, began in 1905, when Captain B.F. Wilson, a Wausau logging contractor, invited Neal Brown, a prominent Wausau lawyer and promoter, to go deer hunting at Star Lake. The deer season of 1905 — the year Wisconsin's Legislature prohibited salt licks and deer hunting with dogs — lasted 20 days and had a two-deer, either-sex bag limit. Wilson and Brown hunted at Camp 28, located in Section 31, north of Lake Laura.

In 1906, Wilson again organized the annual hunt. The party consisted of Neal Brown; C.S. Gilbert; Perry Wilson; A.S. Temple, Milwaukee; M.C. Ewing, the chief official of Wausau's electric utility, who became the camp's crack shot; and M.B. "Caesar" Rosenberry, a judge who became the chief justice of Wisconsin's Supreme Court from 1916 to 1950. In addition, "Ole" Olson was the camp guide; "Old Charlie" Anderson was camp caretaker; and Albert Mykleby, an Arbor Vitae storekeeper, ran the cooking shanty.

The group traveled from Wausau to Star Lake by train and then on horseback to Camp 28, located about three miles northeast of Lake Laura. On the first day of the '06 hunt, crackshot Ewing shot four bucks from the same stand with his .38-caliber Marlin. That stand became known as The Hog's Back. Before the season

ended, Ewing's Marlin burned hot, putting down seven more deer in one day. The party of 11 hunters bagged 13 whitetails that year. In his *History of Deerfoot Lodge* (1941), Rosenberry wrote that deer were plentiful and hunting comparatively easy, because the timber had been recently cut. The deer remained in thickets with open spaces between them.

The grand score for the 1907 hunt at Lake Laura — the year Wisconsin's Legislature prohib-

Rob Wegner Photo Collection.

Deerfoot Lodge, circa 1912.

ited elevated scaffolds for hunting — indicated nine hunters bagged 12 whitetails. The group was equally successful in 1908: 14 hunters got 14 deer; and guide "Ole" Rismon missed a long shot at "Old Tom," the camp's phantom buck that mysteriously appeared and disappeared for years, thus haunting the gentlemen of Deerfoot Lodge.

Such phantom bucks are part of nearly every deer camp in whitetail country. Old Tom, Deerfoot Lodge's buck of mythical proportions,

always eluded his pursuers. Although the 18 regular members of Deerfoot Lodge expended a good amount of ammunition on Old Tom, they never bagged him. No camp members ever became lost in pursuit of Old Tom; they merely became "bewildered," as Rosenberry, the camp's secretary from 1910 to 1935, noted in his history of Deerfoot Lodge.

This page: State Historical Society of Wisconsin. Inset: Rob Wegner Photo Collection.

In his account of Deerfoot Lodge, Rosenberry reported that between 1906 and 1928 members shot 267 deer. This remarkable total occurred at a time when the region's depressed deer herds demanded closed seasons. In *A Century of Wisconsin Deer* (1966), hunting historian Otis Bersing noted that Vilas County had an estimated herd of only 1,600 deer. That population, however, exceeded every other county in the state.

It is difficult to challenge the veracity of the camp secretary's reported tally, however. Let's remember Rosenberry sat on the Wisconsin Supreme Court for 34 years. Rosenberry himself shot 22 deer and won the camp's coveted Big Gun Medal for five years with his biggest deer, a 243-pound buck killed in 1914, the year Jim Jordan shot his world-class buck in Wisconsin's Burnett County. M.C. Ewing, however, reigned supreme at Deerfoot Lodge by taking 43 deer during his time in camp from 1910 to 1935.

In 1909, the hunting party increased to 18 hunters, who shot 17 deer, which included 12 bucks and five does. Deer hunter Perry Wilson emerged as the top gun that year with his 14-pointer. By the end of the season, Ole Olson reported firing a shot at Old Tom a half-mile south of the Hog Pen, but to no avail.

In 1910, the members took up their official residency at Deerfoot

Lodge on the south side of Lake Laura, and shot 23 deer. The camp's log that year indicates a nimrod named Robert Hunter shot an 11-pointer near Deerfoot Lodge that weighed 256 pounds. Hunter's buck scored $191^3/_8$ typical Boone and Crockett points with a $31^1/_2$-inch outside spread, and still stands as Wisconsin's No. 3 typical.

An old woodsman named Charlie Anderson took charge of the property that year, and agreed to live at Deerfoot Lodge year-round. Old Charlie was apparently honest and dependable enough, except that three or four times a year he experienced spells of intense intoxication that generally lasted as long as his money. This strange and somewhat quaint character was never known to touch liquor when deer camp was in session, however. And according to the camp record, "it was Charlie who made Deerfoot Lodge possible, for as caretaker and quasi-host, [he ensured] any member of the Lodge could go there at any time of the year and find a warm shelter, food and a hearty welcome."

The annual hunt at Deerfoot Lodge began Nov. 10 and ended Nov. 30. Generally, 22 men from all walks of life filled the camp's five buildings to capacity when opening day arrived. According to the camp's log, Deerfoot

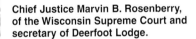

Chief Justice Marvin B. Rosenberry, of the Wisconsin Supreme Court and secretary of Deerfoot Lodge.

Rob Wegner Photo Collection.

In 1909, Deerfoot Lodge increased to 18 hunters who shot 17 deer. Left, an unidentified deerslayer. Above, one of five meatpoles at the lodge sags during the successful 1912 season.

Rob Wegner Photo Collection.

Lodge breakfasts were hearty, consisting of coffee, toast, sausages, potatoes, bread, jam, oranges, apples, hot cakes, camp doughnuts and venison, when available. Even so, there was nothing formal about breakfast. "Some were on time, some were late, some were very late." But all hunters followed Rule No. 1: They were on their stands long before they could see the sights of their rifles.

All meals at Deerfoot Lodge were legendary in and of themselves, as the list of food purchased from J. Mykleby & Son — the Star Lake general store — for the 1911 deer season indicates:

One barrel of flour, three sacks of buckwheat flour, 30 dozen eggs, 65 pounds of sugar, six dozen cans of milk, 30 pounds of lard, 60 pounds of lamb, 21 pounds of bacon, 20 pounds of sausage, 48 pounds of butter, 15 pounds of coffee, 10 pounds of cheese, 10 pounds of salt, 24 cans of jam, one dozen cans of tomatoes, one dozen cans of corn, 25 packages of "better biscuit," 25 pounds of corn meal, five bushels of oats, 25 pounds of cabbage, 12 pounds of carrots, 15 pounds of dry beans, 10 pounds of dry peas, 10 pounds of salt pork, 12 pounds of "beggies," or rutabagas.

Add to that yeast, nutmeg, tea, onions, kerosene, matches, vanilla, ketchup, tablets, envelopes, toothpicks, molasses, napkins, lemons, raisins, currants, ginger snaps, corn starch, carpet tacks, Royal baking powder, one package of Gold Dust, 10 bars of Santa Claus soap, and a dozen rolls of toilet paper. The bill came to $117.40, which is harder to believe than Ewing bagging seven deer in one day!

The 1911 hunt was successful, with the camp shooting 25 deer. But one hunter, Captain Frank Wilson, had an unfortunate time right up until the bottom of the ninth inning. Rosenberry recalled the incident in his camp history:

"In 1911, he had been very unfortunate. He commenced hunting on the first day, continued to the last, and up to the 18th he had not had an opportunity to get his deer. That morning, with the snow from twenty inches to two feet deep, the party set out for the green timber. It was very difficult going. Everyone thought the deer would seek the pines for protection against the storm. We were disappointed and after the drive of the green timber was over most of the party concluded to go back to camp.

"H.A. Patterson, Emil Braatz and myself made up our minds that we would get a shot for Wilson. We took the four best ponies and hunted the remainder of the forenoon and all

These Lake Laura deerslayers at Camp 23 were under the leadership of Presbyterian minister James M. Duer, first from left.

Minnesota Historical Society.

of the afternoon, using the ponies for driving. We put Wilson on the best stations, and while we started a good many deer, none came his way. Wilson was very much hampered in his movements because of a lame knee. He had been at West Baden, Hot Springs and various other places trying to get rid of the neuritis, rheumatism or whatever it was, but he had not had very much success. It was still snowing, the clouds were heavy and dark when a little after four we made up our minds to go back to camp as we did not want to be caught out in the dark in two feet of snow. We were near the Hog Pen about three and one-half miles from camp, when we started for Deerfoot Lodge.

"Wilson led the way, Patterson came next, then Braatz and I brought up the rear with the old gray mare. We were a discouraged lot, tired and a long way from camp with bad weather and very bad footing. We were following an old Brown Brothers road. We had proceeded about a quarter of a mile, when I saw Wilson draw his gun from the scabbard, jump off his pony, sneak along the cut in which we were traveling and commence to shoot.

"He kept shooting and yelling for Emil Braatz. We all dismounted in a jiffy and there was considerable excitement for a few minutes. When it was over, Wilson had his deer, a 225-pound buck, a beautiful animal with a fine head. He told me that was the first good head he had killed, although he had hunted deer all his life and had killed a great many, but the heads were all either small or defective. After the shooting was over, Wilson had been hopping around like a boy. I said to him, 'Frank, how is your leg?' whereupon he grabbed his knee, called to Emil to bring his pony and his old trouble was all back again. He won the Big Gun Medal, which helped some."

The 1912 deer season proved the most successful year in the camp's history. The 22 hunters shot 31 deer — 19 bucks and 12 does — with "Caesar" Rosenberry getting the largest buck, which weighed 205 pounds dressed. (The estimated statewide harvest that year — that is,

deer transported by rail only — reached 5,858.)

Deerfoot Lodge hunters employed two basic methods of hunting: driving and tracking/still-hunting. When driving, six or seven men rode ponies. They were referred to as "the army." Captain Wilson, a delightful camp companion, generally took charge of the expeditions. Rosenberry described the procedures:

"The first drive was generally Brown Brothers Drive as we called it, the jack pine thicket east of Brown Brothers Camp. The second drive was Camp 17 Drive. Sometimes smaller thickets were driven. These drives generally yielded from two to three, sometimes four or five deer. The deer were dressed in the field, that is, the lungs, heart and entrails were removed. By half past eleven, the party which had been driving the thickets assembled either at Camp 15, the Hog Pen or some other agreed point.

"The lone hunters usually came in, a fire was built; each man carried his own luncheon with a small pail for making tea. About an hour was spent in talking over the events of the forenoon, then the party was reorganized into smaller groups of two or three men and the smaller thickets were hunted during the afternoon, the party usually hunting toward camp. When it was convenient to do so, we made an effort to bring in some of the deer, as in this way we were saved making a special trip for them at a later time."

The deer hunt generally ended "around the fire light's ruddy glow," singing the hunting songs of Deerfoot Lodge, one of which was written to the tune "I've Been Working on the Railroad," by associate member James M. Duer, a pastor at Wausau's First Presbyterian Church:

Each fall we go to hunt the deer,
A band of ardent nimrods,
At Deerfoot Lodge we take our cheer,
For standing on the run-way.

A white-tailed buck about to be loaded on the running board of a "Tin Lizzy," circa 1927.

CHORUS

I've been standing on the run-way,
All the live long day;
I've been standing on the run-way,
For a deer to come my way;
Can't you hear the captain's orders,
Rise up so early in the morn,
Can't you hear the captain shouting,
Charlie, blow your horn.

Our ardent hope and fondest dream,
Is bringing down the winner,
As forth we steal at dawn's first gleam,
To stand upon the run-way.

When evening shadows gently climb,
We turn our faces homeward,
And dream of better luck next time,
From Standing on the run-way.

Around the fire light's ruddy glow
We gather close each evening,
And swap our yarns of weal or woe,
From standing on the run-way.

Deerfoot Lodge had a well-articulated set of rules. Some even contained the added dimension of humor. Consider these rules from the camp's log:

"Don't hold mass meetings in the woods any more than you can help. At such meetings there is only a slight attendance of deer. If you have to get together for confab, do it silently like Indians or shadows. After you have killed a deer, look on those that are left dispassionately, not avidly or voraciously; consider the claims of the amateurs who haven't killed a deer and give them a chance. Don't rub it into them by killing more and thus deprive them of their right. Tub in the nearby lake every two or three days, first breaking the ice. Nothing is more conducive to good feeling than this."

Deerfoot Lodge also exercised explicit rules regarding the care and handling of guns: "No one under any circumstances was to bring a loaded gun indoors. No one cleaned or even handled guns in camp except the guides, who carefully examined every gun before cleaning so as to be certain that there were no cartridges remaining in the barrel or the magazine. No one was to shoot at any object until he was certain it was a deer." Deerfoot Lodge never experienced a hunting accident in its 25-year history.

Deerfoot Lodge tended to be family-oriented,

Minnesota Historical Society.

Women were occasionally invited to hunt at Deerfoot Lodge, including the hunter in this photo from 1914.

consisting of several close-knit families who socialized with each other throughout the year, not just during deer season. Because camp members and their sons took up most of the available room, guests were rarely invited. Such an occasion occurred in 1912, however, when Emerson Hough of Chicago, author of *The Covered Wagon* and other classic stories, arrived for deer season at Deerfoot.

And in 1924, Horace Kent Tenney (1859-1932), a prominent Chicago lawyer and legal writer, turned up at Deerfoot Lodge to join his friend Chief Justice Rosenberry. Before returning to Chicago, Tenney presented the lodge an autographed copy of his newly published book *Vert & Venison*, 1924, and read aloud at the dinner table his poem "The Cabin on the Bay":

The huntin' season's comin' on,
I feel the old pulse stir,
I see the leaves a-flutterin' down,
I hear the partridge whirr:
I see the buck's track in the snow,
An' straight my fancies stray
To where the hills look down upon
A cabin on a bay.
Oh! it's huntin' up the Mink Run Road,
An' peerin' all around,
An' seein' every thing that moves,
An' hearin' every sound:
An' trailin' where Mount Ida's top
Salutes the comin' day,
An' trudgin' back at nightfall to
The cabin on the bay.
The crooked runway's windin' line
Invites my willin' feet,
'Twas made by those who never knew
The trammels of a street:
By woods an' hills an' lakes an' rills
It leads its steadfast way,
An' those who foot it know full well
The cabin on the bay.
Oh! its huntin' up the Cliff Lake trails,
An' seein' every track,
An' throwin' up your rifle quick
An' hearin' it go crack:

Postcard dated 1909.

Rob Wegner Photo Collection.

An' cuttin' poles to hang him up,
The only proper way —
An' tellin' all about it
In the cabin on the bay.
What though the city's noisy streets
Confine our steps today,
'Tis not for long, an' soon we'll see
The cabin on the bay.

Although Deerfoot Lodge was male-dominated, women occasionally hunted there as guests, including a Minnesota woman in 1914 with a highly cherished double-barrel shotgun. Her picture circulated through Deerfoot Lodge memorabilia in several states.

Each summer, Deerfoot Lodge members held their annual meeting dressed in formal attire. These meetings produced some of the best American deer and deer hunting tales ever told.

The present-day deer camp hasn't changed much in that regard. According to two University of Wisconsin sociologists, strong family ties are not only a key factor in developing and sustaining an interest in deer hunting, but also influence deer-camp traditions. One deer hunter, for example, made the point this way: "My father not only taught us to be hunters, (he also taught) my cousins. Together, we make a party of seven who all hunt the same way, think the same, and wait all year to be together for the deer hunt."

This sense of togetherness and camaraderie remains an essential ingredient of the American deer camp, and reveals itself in this entry in the camp's log, which was written in response to the death of M.C. "Crack Shot" Ewing:

"In the death of M.C. Ewing, Deerfoot Lodge suffered an irreparable loss and there is left a vacancy which can never be filled. Perhaps there is no better test of genuineness of character than the trials and hardships of deer camp and no place where men more freely and unreservedly disclose their true character. In the field and around the campfire, he contributed his full share of all that goes to make friendship and companionship really worthwhile. His solicitude for the welfare of others, and his vast knowledge of the habits and ways of the wild, all found full scope for exercise and made him in deer camp, as everywhere, a leader."

The story of Deerfoot Lodge came to a close with declining deer densities and the deaths of many loyal members. The liquidation of the lodge, one of the great deer hunting meccas of the North Woods, occurred in Fall 1935. The last nostalgic entry in the camp's log reveals what deer camp means to American deer hunters.

"There probably will never be another Deerfoot Lodge, or anything like it for our crowd, and it does hurt to have it pass out of our lives. Of course, we cannot be deprived of our deer camp memories and we can treasure them for the balance of the time we are permitted to strive for existence and struggle with the Depression. Deerfoot Lodge really made a record and brought everyone of us closer together.

"Today the old Lodge is the happy abode of its new owners, who have made it gay with awnings, window boxes and screen porches and very livable with the refinements of running water, modern kitchen equipment, and beds with inner-spring mattresses. If with nostalgic longing the shades of Captain Wilson and 'Old Charlie' bringing with them from the Happy Hunting Grounds 'Old Tom' the deer ... not one of them would recognize their old haunts. They would turn sadly away, disappearing through the pines, never to return. For Deerfoot Lodge as they knew it, is no more."

A popular Remington advertisement seen in hunting magazines during the Deerfoot Lodge era, circa 1916.

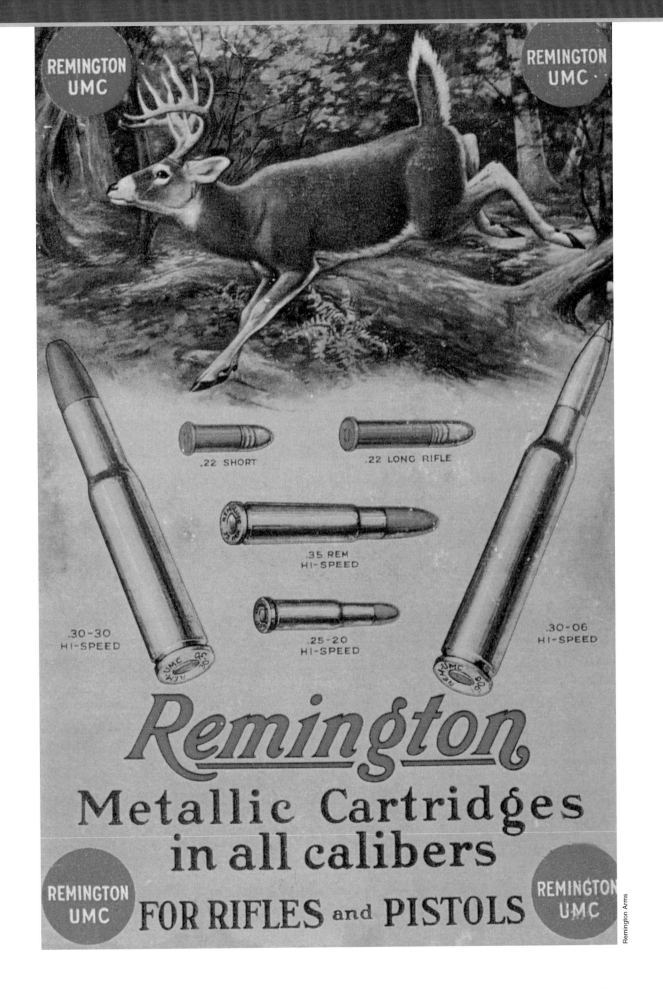

REMINGTON UMC

REMINGTON UMC

.22 SHORT

.22 LONG RIFLE

.35 REM HI-SPEED

.30-30 HI-SPEED

.25-20 HI-SPEED

.30-06 HI-SPEED

Remington
Metallic Cartridges
in all calibers
FOR RIFLES and PISTOLS

REMINGTON UMC

REMINGTON UMC

Remington Arms

HE BUCKS CAMP
OURNAL

"Every November, when the hunting fever began stirring the blood, the members headed for the hills. Doctors, lawyers, dentists, bankers, ministers (to identify a few) dropped everything and left for the woods to hunt deer."

— *The Bucks Camp Log*
1916-1928

The Bucks Camp. 1913. Rob Wegner Photo Collection.

I n Fall 1913, a group of avid buck hunters from Ladysmith, Wis., banded together and created the Bucks Camp club. These hunters loved to chase whitetails and prided themselves on their woodsmanship. In November that year, they built a tar-paper shack on 160 acres of Rusk County wilderness on the eastern shore of Lake Stephenson — now called Star Lake — south of Deer Lake and Deer Creek. Every fall, when deer hunting fever stirred their blood, the Bucks Camp members dropped everything and headed for their Blue Hills deer shack with a persistence matched only by Jack Frost.

Marjorie Williams, daughter of Judge Glenn H. Williams — a perennial member and keeper of the club's records — describes the scene:

"As a youngster I was always mystified and awed by this November ritual of deer hunting and the inevitable exodus to Bucks Camp. Several weeks before the event took place, my father began to acquire a kind of glow, and the smell of gun oil and rubber boots hung in the air. An object referred to as a pack sack was brought forth and filled with wool socks, flannel shirts, and more to the point, I thought, a big bar of German sweet chocolate for quick energy in case he got lost in the woods. I knew what happened on the home front while the men were off on this hunting foray. My mother locked more doors than usual; we got to sleep later, and all the neighborhood women and children gathered for a manless Thanksgiving dinner."

The highlight of the Bucks Camp was an old leather-bound ledger book, originally found in a dusty attic 50 years after its last entry dated Dec. 9, 1928. This deer-camp diary, discovered in the possessions of Judge Williams, revealed the true and ageless spirit of the deer hunt, and includes everything from tragedy to exciting adventures, and humor, woodsmanship and philosophical reflections on the nature of hunting.

The diary, published as *The Bucks Camp Log, 1916-1928* (1974), also contains poetry and satir-

The Bucks score on Thanksgiving Day, 1920.

Minnesota Historical Society.

ical, extemporaneous dissertations by attorney and camp-member L.E. McGill. This witty and skillful writer, known as "Stump Fire Ranger," presumably wrote most of the text. Here is one of his deer-camp dissertations, written in memory of the "Bucks" he loved:

In Memoriam

The Bucks are dead; please call the hearse.
They long have been cold; it couldn't be worse.
Once they stood like strong and virile men,
But that is a story of what might have been.
They discarded their guns for lipstick red.
Why wonder then that their souls have fled?
Once they were active and together were strong.
But with powder and puff they all went wrong.
Their interest and action gave way to words,
And they twittered away like sparrow birds.

David Kowalski.

Winchester rifles, cartridges and paintings by Lynn Bogue Hunt are synonymous with white-tailed deer hunting and deer camp, especially the Bucks Camp. This artwork was produced between 1906 and 1915.

They deserted the places and things they loved well,
To follow a trail that they thought more swell.
These poor old Bucks who once held sway,
With foible and fashion they fell by the way.
Like David of old they lay without heat,
Nor all of the virgins could e'en warm their feet.
So step gently, friend, and pull the shroud,
For in Life these Bucks were very proud.

This deer hunting diary also contains historical photographs and a detailed hand-drawn map of their cherished hunting grounds, which came from the original camp log. As a result, we're able to sample the authentic flavor of this Wisconsin deer camp in northwestern

Rusk County.

Whether the bucks ran crooked or straight, the hunters claimed they could "shoot the whiskers off a wood tick by way of pastime," as Stump Fire Ranger wrote in the diary Nov. 28, 1926.

The diary begins with a description of Wisconsin's deer season in 1917, the year the state first required deer tags, which cost 10 cents apiece. That year, 53,593 deer hunting licenses were sold. Thirteen hunters arrived in camp Nov. 20 that year. When the season closed nine days later, nine bucks graced the Bucks Camp meatpole. Wisconsin estimated that its 1917 statewide deer harvest reached 18,000.

Despite the hunters' ample skills, they still confronted that disease known as buck fever. In an entry dated Nov. 25, 1917, Stump Fire Ranger reported this disease especially affected Mr. Elmer W. Hill Sr., pioneer Apollonia resident, store merchant and Rusk County clerk of courts:

"The bunch drove the vicinity of Poise Stump this afternoon. Mr. E. W. Hill Sr. was feeling well enough to join the bunch. A lead mine could be started with the bullets we left down there. We had five deer surrounded. The bombardment sounded like an English barrage. Deer were running everywhere. They were so thick around Mr. Hill Sr. that he had to push them away beyond the end of his gun so he could shoot them. He got buck fever so bad that he was shooting in a circle. Mr. True said the air was so thick around Mr. Hill Sr. that he could not shoot through it."

Before the 1917 hunt ended, Stump Fire Ranger acknowledged Nov. 23 that the camp's in-house pastor, the Rev. Mielecki of Kelner, Wis., neither took a drink nor swore that day.

Baked beans and raisin pie highlighted the menu for the 1918 deer hunt. Thirteen loyal Bucks returned to camp that season, the year in which the Wisconsin Legislature protected fawns. Five bucks went to the Bucks Camp meatpole.

Apparently, Elmer Hill was not the only camp member suffering from buck fever. J.W. Carow also fought the infernal disease, as we learn from the Nov. 27, 1918, entry:

"Oh, I am a crack shot" says Carow
At sixty yards I can hit a sparrow
"But when at buck and doe
A box of bullets I throw
I can't hit the side of a wheelbarrow."

But the Bucks cured that disease, and soon had their share of personal triumphs. For example, Dr. W.F. O'Connor — pioneer Tony-Ladysmith physician — shot a 12-point buck on Nov. 26, 1918. He shot the buck at the head of "The Big Ravine," hitting it in the right eye on a dead run. That night in camp, his hunting buddy Hank Davis proudly announced:

"O'Connor is the expert guy
He takes them standing I cannot lie
He slaps a cripple on the rump

David Kowalski.

And makes him jump
Then hits him in the opposite eye."

As the Bucks' campfire blazed that night, the distinguished Dr. O'Connor — known as the cocky Irishman — kept bragging how, why and where he killed his buck. After imbibing a generous amount of spirits, the doctor so stretched his lies that Davis turned from the campfire and yelled: "Hell, Doc, don't stretch that out any longer. I've lost all chance of heaven now trying to back you up!"

Dr. O'Connor stood up, sipped his Irish whiskey, stared at Davis and warned everyone in camp to stay the hell out of Lone Pine Country, because he was going down there tomorrow to get another 12-pointer with an eye shot. As the embers died and howls of timber wolves drifted through the pines, the Bucks drifted off to sleep.

In 1919, 13 Bucks returned to the tar-paper shack on Lake Stephenson to resume the chase and eat Herman's delicious, invigorating buckwheat cakes. On Nov. 26, a cold and windy day, L.C. Streater — a Ladysmith banker — jumped a nice buck out of a swamp. After shooting four times, he admitted "he didn't know they could run so crooked!"

The hunters of the Bucks Camp were compatible by nature and willing to share workloads. The right human chemistry is needed to make a deer camp function, and the Bucks Camp was a classic example of the proper mix. Their camaraderie was not only evident in the field, but also at the card table. Aside from the guns, knives, hunting licenses and red clothing, the most important requirement at the Bucks Camp was a pocketful of nickels. These deer-camp card games — whether smear, poker or sheepshead — were played in earnest, as we learn from this

diary entry:

"Le Blanc got us up at 5:30 a.m. for pancakes. Everybody sat down just as though they were real deer hunters, and the pancakes disappeared. Then most of the bunch calmly received the report of some hardy soul that the day outside was a little unpleasant and decided not to venture out into the inclement weather, but got their exercise playing smear."

While this log entry likely contains more humor than fact, it seems evident the hunters played many games of smear, and that they passed around sundry libations during these games. Their policy on drinking, however, was summarized in one word: moderation.

With the return of soldiers from World War I, the 1920 Wisconsin deer season proved successful statewide. The harvest reached 20,025, an all-time high in those days, with 69,479 deer hunters taking part.

Although selling venison was and remains

Minnesota Historical Society.

Always dressed in style, Minnesota deer hunter John Herricks, above, frequently hunted at the Bucks Camp. Circa 1919. Left, the old Knapp Stout Co. cabin built in 1878 north of Buck's Road, circa 1922. Note its skylight.

Rob Wegner Photo Collection.

illegal, many resorts in northern Wisconsin had venison on their menus during deer season, which delighted hunters.

The 1920 season also brought the first use of metal tags in Wisconsin, which sold for 25 cents. The bag limit that year was one buck with antlers not less than 3 inches long. When opening day arrived Nov. 21, 1920, 16 hunters arrived at the Bucks Camp. Despite statewide success, only one of the Bucks Camp's hunters shot a buck. The camp log documents the problem:

"It (the opening day) was the wettest known here. Rained, snowed and sleeted off and on all day. What hunting was done was of no avail. ... Deer are reported plentiful — five miles away. None were seen today. ... No deer killed today. ... If someone doesn't get a buck tomorrow, Streater says, there will be no Thanksgiving. And that is good gospel. ... Elmer got three shots at a buck, but too much brush."

An entry dated Nov. 26 indicated F.M. Doyle came in for dinner with several deer hunting rumors, as usual. One was a report that someone had shot game warden Lewis Soyle while hunting north of Ingram. Another rumor concerned a 17-year-old boy named Walt Kittleson, who reportedly downed a giant 24-point buck near Seeley with a Winchester Model 94 in a .32 Special on Nov. 21. That rumor proved accurate. Kittleson's buck scores 218⁴/₈ Boone and Crockett points. Without the side tines, it would measure 212 typical. It currently stands as the state's No. 20 nontypical.

The Bucks Camp Log, 1916-1928, has an entry from Nov. 22, 1920, that depicts the camp's spirit of play and camaraderie:

"These short-tailed Bucks are a suspicious bunch. If this Log isn't written in every night, they imagine they will suffer the punishment of poor hunting when they cross over Jordan.

"This is the year of the 'One Buck Law.' Length of horn must be three inches. Diligent search was made, reports and confessions received from which it appears that no Buck in camp can qualify except Davis. On account of this superior qualification, he is becoming very disagreeable. A secret conference has decided he must be dehorned.

"O'Connor still talks about 'shooting them in the eye', but stays in camp nursing an infected wrist and eating more than half the crew.

"Blackburn and Doyle left yesterday, and it is reported that Billy will return when he gets a change of underwear.

"Davis, Davis, sixty years old today!
May he live another hundred
For we all enjoy his play
Young in body, mind and spirit
Shedding sunshine all the way
A friend of sterling worth and merit
May he never pass away."

Some of the Bucks with nine deer, 1923.

Minnesota Historical Society.

Minnesota Historical Society.

O n Nov. 12, 1921, 15 hunters showed up for supper at the shack. The deer tag that year cost 25 cents. The 1921 deer hunt proved snowy, extremely cold and unsuccessful, as evidenced by one entry:

"The Last of the Mohicans still hunt, but with less speed than usual as the snow is nearly up to the second joint above the ankle of the average Buck."

The fact that success eluded the Bucks in 1921 comes as no surprise, for the status of Wisconsin's deer herd that year was bleak. Game officials feared for the herd's very survival.

"Deer are destined sooner or later to cease to be a game animal in Wisconsin," said the 1921-22 report of the Conservation Department. "Civilization is crowding them farther and farther back in narrower quarters, and hunters are increasing in number each year, all of which casts a gloomy horoscope for the future of the once-abundant game animals in Wisconsin."

In 1922, the Bucks moved their deer camp to an abandoned logging cabin north of Buck's Road. The cabin — built in 1878 by the Knapp Stout Co. — was located on the shore of what is now called Bucks Lake. The Stump Fire Ranger reported in his poem "Buck's Day," that the new campsite allowed the Bucks to commune with the cosmos and the gods of good cheer.

In 1923, the Bucks saw 11 deer but killed only one. The 1924 deer season proved more successful, with four bucks gracing their meatpole. The statewide buck harvest that year reached 7,000.

In 1925, the Wisconsin Legislature closed deer season and initiated alternate-year closed and buck-only seasons. However, the Bucks still went to camp in 1925 to fish, hunt grouse, and repair the log cabin.

When deer season reopened in 1926 — the

When Wisconsin closed the deer season in 1925 and 1927, the Bucks still returned to camp to hunt grouse.

year William Monypeny Newsom published his popular book *White-tailed Deer*, which was read by many club members, 17 Bucks came to camp and filled all 17 beds. Only two white-tailed bucks went on the meatpole, however. One was shot by L.E. McGill and the other by Joe "Big Buck" McCorrison.

The season was closed again in 1927, and the '28 deer season opened Dec. 1. The deer tag now cost 50 cents, and all hunters were required to wear an official conservation button while hunting. Fifteen Bucks returned to camp and outwitted seven white-tailed bucks.

On Dec. 6, McGill — the Stump Fire Ranger — recorded a fine example of stealthy deer behavior:

"This morning we were standing on the brink of the ravine called the 'canal' by our boys, and we were treated to an example of deer woodcraft which was wonderful.

"Hoping to waylay an unsuspecting buck which attempted to cross, we had taken our station on the rim of this valley. After 15 minutes of waiting, we heard a twig break. We turned our heads and looked into the eyes of a doe standing alert about 200 feet away. Behind her was a little fawn. She surveyed us intently for several minutes. Finally she decided we were not dangerous but, just the same, a little more distance would be advisable. She turned and proceeded away from us a short distance; the fawn following close behind. She then turned and carefully surveyed us again. We had not moved and the wind was toward us. She was satisfied with us and now gave her attention to the perilous journey across the 'valley-of-the-shadow-of-death.' Before venturing, she looked carefully in every direction, tested the air with her nose and listened with her large ears erect. After a careful inspection, she twitched her tail and proceeded down the side of the ravine, the fawn standing immovable.

A WISCONSIN DEER CAMP DIARY:

The Bucks Camp Log

1916-1928

A WISCONSIN DEER CAMP DIARY

The original Bucks Camp log was reproduced in book form in 1974 by the *Wisconsin Sportsman* magazine and reprinted in 1989 by Willow Creek Press. Both editions of *The Bucks Camp Log, 1916-1928*, are out of print. An original 1974 edition with its dust jacket was selling for $75 in 2001 in the out-of-print book market.

This book is, as publisher Tom Petrie noted, "an extraordinary inside look at the character of early 20th century deer hunters: their daily camp life, their humor, their camp's wilderness surroundings ... The modern-day deer hunter will find much in this diary that might have been written just last deer season, and will recognize many of the personalities — with different names, from a different time — of his own hunting partners."

Rob Wegner Photo Collection.

"Two Bucks and a Doe." A postcard from the era of the Bucks Camp.

The doe went down the slope very carefully and slowly one foot at a time; eyes, ears and nose on the alert for man, the killer. Her progress was like a slow-motion picture of a thoroughbred race horse, knees high, head erect. When she reached the bottom of the ravine, at a signal we missed, the fawn came down to her. Still alert, she then started across the floor of the valley-of-the-shadow. The fawn, at a signal, joined her and together they quickly went up the side and out of sight.

"It was as beautiful a piece of woodcraft as we have ever seen, careful, cautious, silent, scientific. The only mistake was the first brush crack. Except for that, we would not have seen the crossing. For a buck, this error would have been fatal. During the journey, we were as anxious for their safety as was the old doe. We felt ourselves mentally urge her to hurry. When the deer was gone — we hate to admit it — there was a lump in our throats, and we wanted to call to the doe and tell her that the valley-of-the-shadow was not a dangerous place, but the safest refuge in the world."

Although the Wisconsin deer population was at an all-time low during the Bucks Camp's existence of 1913 to 1928, the one-buck law and alternate-year hunts helped rebuild the herd in the years following that era.

Memories of the Bucks Camp and its romantic places — High Bridge Green, the Big Ravine, Day's Pine, Lone Pine Country and Poise Hill Stump — will live forever in the minds of deer hunters. Not only do such memories provide a fascinating glimpse of the past, but they remind us of grand deer-camp traditions that constitute our great deer-hunting heritage.

OPOLD
NG AT THE SHACK

"To the deer hunter or the outdoorsman, deer are the inner meaning of forested terrain. Their presence or absence does not affect the outward appearance of the forest, but does mightily affect our reaction toward it. Without deer tracks in the trail and the potential presence of deer at each new dip and bend of the trail, the forest would be, to the outdoorsman, an empty shell, a spiritual vacuum."

— *Aldo Leopold*

Painting by Owen Kampen. Courtesy of the National Wildlife Federation.

Aldo Leopold was born in 1887, the year Theodore Roosevelt founded the Boone and Crockett Club, a conservation organization that Leopold later joined as an associate member. After graduating from Yale University with a master's degree in forestry in 1909, the 22-year-old hunter/naturalist took a job with the U.S. Forest Service in the Southwest as a forest assistant. As he traveled the Apache National Forest in the Arizona territory during the early 20th century, Leopold read Roosevelt's *Outdoor Pastimes of an American Hunter*, campaigned for public deer hunting grounds in the national forest, and gave lectures on hunting ethics to sportsmen's organizations.

Between 1909 and 1924, Leopold rode thousands of miles on horseback over the national forests, many of them on a feisty gray stallion called Jiminy Hicks. Dressed in leather and looking like Thad Eburne of Buckskin Mountain, the main character of Zane Grey's *The Deer Stalker* (1925), Leopold shot deer with his Winchester .30-30 Model '94 and ate venison steak cooked on open fires. His romantic cowboy existence resembled in many ways that of Theodore Roosevelt decades earlier, whom Leopold saw as a model of heroic stature.

When not inspecting trees, marking them for cutting, planting seed plots and fixing fences, Leopold hunted deer, climbed mountains and tested trout streams. His backwoods hunting camps often consisted of an improvised lean-to, a back-woods ranger shack or a natural rock ledge, as depicted in Charlie Russell's oil painting "Man's Weapons are Useless When Nature Goes Armed" (1916), one of Leopold's favorite prints.

When the New Mexico deer season opened Nov. 20, 1923, Aldo and his wife, Estella, left for a pack trip into the interior of the Gila Wilderness Area. They rode on horseback up Black Canyon and pitched their deer camp on Diamond Creek. On the first day of the hunt, they saw many white-tailed does but few bucks.

"Over the oak coals of the campfire each evening, we held a council of war," Leopold wrote.

Finally, on the fifth day Aldo saw two white-tailed bucks, but after two shots from his Model '94 Winchester, one vanished behind a Douglas fir and the other into heavy brush. While returning to camp at sundown, he came up over a pine mesa. He records the following event in his 1923 hunting journal:

"I suddenly saw a big white-tailed deer standing broadside to me by an oak tree. Couldn't see any horns but put the glasses on him and immediately saw he had very good ones. He was directly against the sun and hard to make out. Dropped to my knees and found both an oak limb and the grass tops in my way but there was no time to be lost so I let fly. He didn't move — I must have shot over. I again fired quickly and this time he went down."

The 8-point whitetail weighed more than 200 pounds.

Carl Leopold at the Whiterock Deer Camp, 1929, with his Winchester '94 in .30-30.

University of Wisconsin-Madison Archives.

Leopold's passion for deer hunting is recorded on almost every page of his hunting journals. In Fall 1926, Leopold became interested in hunting deer with the bow and arrow — undoubtedly a result of reading Saxton Pope's 1925 edition of *Hunting with the Bow and Arrow*. Pope and Arthur Young became the founding fathers of modern bow-hunting.

From that point forward, Leopold read and collected many famous books on the history and theory of archery and bow-hunting. His library on this subject featured many classic titles, including everything from Ascham's *Toxophilus* to Thompson's *The Witchery of Archery*. He also read and studied William Monypeny Newsom's *White-tailed Deer* and Roosevelt's *The Deer Family*, taking extensive notes from these classic texts on deer hunting methodology.

One of Leopold's first deer hunting trips with the bow occurred in 1927, when he and Howard Weiss — treasurer of the C.F. Burgess Laboratories — hunted whitetails and blacktails in New Mexico's Gila National Forest, an area Leopold had studied as a forester. The day they left for the hunt, *The Chicago Daily Tribune* announced optimistically that they were expected to bring home at least a deer apiece, because of their considerable experience and expertise with bows and arrows.

Their deer hunting enthusiasm ran high. As Leopold wrote in his hunting journal, "We're going to rimrock those bucks on the battleground of New Mexico!" He estimated the population at 38 deer per square mile.

They set up camp under two large pines near a spring covered with watercress in the Mogollon Mountains upriver from Canyon Creek and beneath Loco Mountain Mesa. They were soon stalking deer in an endless maze of box canyons. After several days of diligent hunting and heartbreaking misses, their persistence waned.

As with Pope and Young, these early-vintage bow-hunters were long-range shooters. Leopold gives us an example:

"One large whitetail looked at me at seventy yards. He jumped at the flash of the bow. My arrow stuck in his second jump, so that if he had stood still I would have hit him fairly in the neck."

On Nov. 13, Leopold returned to deer camp by following a high mesa rim. In his hunting journal, he recalls what he saw:

"Walking along this high prairie in the somber sunset with a howling wind tossing the old cedars along the rim, and a soaring raven croaking over the abyss below, was a solemn and impressive experience. Jumped three whitetails right out on the prairie, but it was too late to see horns. They were very pretty bounding over the sea of yellow grama grass with the wind blowing them along like tufts of thistledown."

Their enthusiasm suffered a stunning blow when Leopold hit a large buck, but failed in his three-day effort to recover it. In his journal he noted they experienced several blue evenings in camp.

"I saw the buck in a pine thicket at fifty yards. I moved to avoid a bush, drew to the barb at point blank, and let fly. The unmistakable thud of the arrow striking flesh told me I had hit — as nearly as I could tell — in the fore ribs or shoulder. The buck plunged like a pitching bronco and disappeared over the hogback."

Their confidence and ambition returned, however, with clean underwear and warm sunshine.

Although Leopold was unsuccessful in his efforts to get a deer on this trip, he formulated some proverbs for deer camp discussion:

"(1) Some whitetails stay in oaks regardless of nuts; (2) Bucks do not necessarily bed on the same side of a canyon they feed on; (3) Only does water before dark, but both bucks and does feed before dark; (4) When you stop to look, stop in the shade; (5) Deer cannot be stalked in dry country except in a heavy wind or early morning. North slopes stay quiet longest; (6) A startled deer will tend to go (a) uphill, (b) into the wind, (c) around a point, (d) toward cover or rough ground. When he is startled by sight, (letter b) is the strongest tendency, when by scent any of the others may be."

Springerville, Arizona Territory, 1909. Young Aldo Leopold in full cowboy regalia as he hunts black-tailed bucks for camp meat for his 1909 reconnaissance crew.

Leopold remained determined to return to the Gila National Forest to continue the chase. In 1929, the chase resumed in earnest when Leopold, his son Starker and his brother Carl again returned to this wilderness hunting grounds. They again found deer wonderfully abundant. On opening day, Carl got an 11-point, 175-pound buck in Buck Canyon with his .30-30 Model '94. Leopold, meanwhile, brought his 60-pound Osage bow and six dozen Alaska cedar arrows with Weniger broadheads. The high quantity of arrows reminds us again of the early adventures of Pope and Young.

The Leopold party backpacked into an area east of Aldo's 1927 campsite and set up camp under the flanks of Black Mountain in an area known as the Whiterock Tank Region. This campsite offered a magnificent view:

"The whole immensity of the Gila basin lay spread before us in a sunset so quiet you could hear a cricket chirp. It was a sight worth the whole trip."

Their camp became known as the Whiterock Deer Camp, and Carl's 11-pointer soon provided them with venison jerky and kidney stew.

The Leopolds' daily campaigns generally consisted of two men driving with one man standing. Success with this method depended on knowing which localities were susceptible to driving. As Leopold acknowledged: "We frequently wasted half of our time trying to drive undrivable lay-outs. An indefinite amount of time could be well-invested in advance in finding the lay-outs which actually work."

Small drives for deer, Leopold believed, were useless unless they proceeded slowly enough for each man to sit half the time.

During their 10-day hunt they saw more than 200 deer, with does outnumbering bucks 3-to-1. On the next-to-last day of their hunt, Leopold saw three deer descending a hill toward him through

University of Wisconsin Archives.

heavy brush near Whitetail Point. He wrote:

"When directly opposite me, and about sixty yards distant, they stopped, seemed to ponder the fate of nations, and then to my utter surprise, plunged squarely down the hill and directly at me, but still obscured by brush. As they filed across a small opening I made out that the first two were does, while the last seemed to be a spiker. I drew on a clear opening under a juniper where I knew they would pass, about thirty yards to my left, and in a moment the two does filed by in that peculiar hesitating trot which makes it uncertain whether the next instant will bring a total stop or a terrified leap. Then came the spiker. I was not yet sure whether his horns were six inches (the legal minimum), and devoted the first instant of clear vision to verifying this fact instead of to a final appraisal of distance and aim, as I should have. Then I shot. The arrow passed over his back and splintered harmlessly on the rocks. ... More perfect chances to make a kill do not occur, except in deer hunters' dreams."

According to Leopold's 1929 journal, mealtime ceremonies at their deer camp were special occasions. For example, on the day they arrived, Leopold wrote:

"We dined on a pot of beans and corn bread in a fall of snow which started in the middle of the afternoon and by bedtime was two inches deep. Had music in our snug dry camp after dinner while all the rest of the world outside was white and cold."

The next evening they dined on ham, hominy and sourdough biscuits. Their menu during this trip included everything from venison liver, heart and kidney stew to turkey legs, quail and roasted venison ribs over oak coals.

"What one can cook on oak coals is almost unbelievable," Leopold once said.

The ultimate deer camp cuisine was a Leopold treat at the Whiterock Deer Camp. His recipe reads as follows:

"Kill a mast-fed buck, not earlier than November, not later than January. Hang him in a live-oak tree for seven frosts and seven suns. Then cut out the half-frozen straps from their bed of tallow under the saddle, and slice them transversely into steaks. Rub each steak with salt, pepper and flour. Throw into a Dutch oven containing hot, deep-smoking bear fat and standing on live-oak coals. Fish out the steaks at the first sign of browning. Throw a little flour into the fat, then ice-cold water, then milk. Lay a steak on the summit of a steaming sour-dough biscuit and drown both in gravy."

After suppers with menus like this, the Leopolds generally spent their evenings planning the morning's campaign. Later, the "glee club" usually tuned up and got a workout before taking a final belt of cherry bounce and retiring for the night to dream of oak thickets alive with bounding bucks.

After two weeks of chasing deer in the mountainous terrain of New Mexico in 1929, Leopold

Leopold sits on a rimrock on the Perdida Mesa above a tributary of the Gavilan River in northwestern Chihuahua, Mexico, 1938, while pursuing the Sonoran white-tailed deer.

returned to Madison, Wis., and formulated the following maxims of deer hunting:

"(1) A deer never follows anything; (2) A deer will not jump from scent except close by, but he will sneak out as far as the scent will carry; (3) The opposite hillside is always less brushy than the side you are on; (4) Clean your binoculars daily and never hunt without them. Good illumination and clean lenses are necessary to discern antlers in the shadows. Examine every doe twice; (5) Don't be too cautious. You can run up on a trotting or jumping deer, where you couldn't move a foot on a standing or sneaking deer without detection."

In 1934, a historic event occurred in Wisconsin, when the state's Conservation Commission revised hunting laws as a result of Leopold's initiative to include the bow as a legal hunting weapon for deer. Thus, when the Legislature declared a five-day "open season" for deer in Sauk and Columbia counties in 1934, Wisconsin became the first state to establish a bow-hunting season for deer.

According to Otis Bersing, a Wisconsin deer hunting historian, 40 bow-hunters participated in the '34 hunt. Leopold's party of eight constituted 20 percent of those archers! In *Fifteen Years of Bow & Arrow Deer Hunting in Wisconsin* (1949), Bersing reported: "Participants were a small group, viewed tolerably, often looked upon as queer, and at times ridiculed. They reported a kill of one lone buck. Since 1934, with the exception of 1935, when all deer seasons were closed, Wisconsin has had an annual season."

(By 2001, Wisconsin was annually selling more than 230,000 bow licenses, and had an average bow harvest of 78,648 from 1996 to 2000.)

On opening day of the '34 bow-hunt, *The Chicago Daily News* reported, "The whiz of iron-pointed, feather-tipped shafts replaced the roar of shotguns in two counties of central Wisconsin, where for the first time since white men borrowed the country from the Indians, archers are pursuing deer to the exclusion of men with firearms."

Leopold's 1934 deer hunts took place on the sandy Wisconsin River bottomlands near Baraboo, Wis.

Leopold cooking venison tenderloins at "the Shack."

University of Wisconsin-Madison Archives.

Sid Richardson Collection of Western Art, Fort Worth, Texas.

The eight archers at Leopold's deer camp included four family members and several Leopold colleagues from the University of Wisconsin. All of them slept on straw beds in Leopold's 10-by-12-foot army tent despite heavy rains. They ate breakfast and dinner in the dark and lunch in the hills.

During the first two days of the hunt, they tried to locate deer in the lowlands, which were full of tracks. On the third day they discovered deer were bedding in the uplands several miles away. They began driving the upland country and had instant results. They spotted 40 deer, including many bucks. They learned a lesson immediately:

"We found that the does and young deer could be driven with some accuracy and precision, but the bucks were unpredictable. When jumped, they were just as likely to take out across the open fields or sand dunes as through the woods."

During this five-day, landmark bow-hunt, Leopold and his two sons saw 12 bucks, 20 antlerless deer and nine fawns. According to a Leopold biographer, "Their arrows flew wide, far, narrow and short. But they had a rousing good time."

The Leopold party got five shots, two of which came to Leopold. His first chance was a running shot at a medium-sized buck at about 40 yards in dense timber. Apparently, his elevation was right, but he shot just in front of it. His second shot went over the shoulder of a standing 5-by-5 trophy. "The biggest white-tailed buck I have ever seen."

Magnificent antlers always fascinated Leopold. As an associate member of the Boone and Crockett Club, he closely followed reports of trophy deer as they were recorded across North America. During most of Leopold's life, the James G. Brewster buck — which fell to a Model '94 Winchester in 1905 in British Columbia — ranked No. 1 in the world. Leopold's personal copy of the 1939 B&C record book lists Brewster's 26-pointer atop the charts with its widest spread at 33½ inches.

Man's Weapons are Useless When Nature Goes Armed (Weapons of the Weak; Two of a Kind Win.) Oil on Canvas. Charles A. Russell, 1916. Leopold frequently used rocky ledges for backwoods camps as illustrated in this humorous illustration.

After the Leopolds' groundbreaking '34 hunt, however, Aldo was having second thoughts about tent-camping. The rains that fell during the hunt rekindled his yearning for a more permanent deer camp.

In 1935, Leopold acquired an abandoned, worn-out shack near Baraboo to be his base of operations for deer hunting. He originally referred to it as the *Jagdschloss*, or hunting lodge, and later as simply, "the Shack."

This beloved shack has helped many hunters find their meat from God. It also had an outhouse. My friend the late Bob McCabe, noted: "The outhouse, dubbed 'the Parthenon,' was even less pretentious than the Shack. It would have been dangerous to occupy this comfort station in high winds. Near its entrance and wired to a post was a bleached cow skull, the cranium of which acted as a wren house. Not every privy has a vocalist-in-residence."

While vacationing at this antique chicken coop — now on the National Register of Historic Places — Leopold made a yew bow for his friend and colleague Herbert Stoddard, a specialist in quail research. In a letter to Stoddard in January 1935, Leopold revealed his deep-rooted enthusiasm for deer hunting. He wrote:

"One cannot fashion a stave without indulging in fond hopes of its future. On many a thirsty noon I hope you lean it against a mossy bank by cool springs. In fall I hope its shafts will sing in sunny glades where turkeys dwell, and that one day some wily buck will have just long enough to startle at the twang of its speeding string."

In a Jan. 11, 1935, letter to Roy Case — a prominent American bow-hunter who hunted with Leopold at the shack, Aldo acknowledged there is no sport superior to bow-hunting for deer. However, he knew well the frustration bow-hunters encounter while pursuing whitetails:

"Killing a white-tailed buck with a bow and arrow means going through a series of unexpected mishaps and keeping it up until one of the haps fails to miss."

This statement, we must remember, was made by an instinctive shooter of the straight bow in the absence of modern technological equipment.

The shack soon became Leopold's greatest possession. It was a sacred place to meditate and reflect, and "a weekend refuge from too much modernity." Here he penned some of the greatest thoughts ever written on white-tailed deer. From his shack he habitually watched a particular deer trail for years. He eventually cut some brush so he could widen his zone of visibility. He called "the new deer swath" to the attention of weekend guests. After years of observing their responses to the trail and deer activities on it, Leopold categorized four types of outdoorsmen:

"Deer hunters, duck hunters, bird hunters and

Rob Wegner Photo Collection.

nonhunters. These categories have nothing to do with sex or age, or accouterments; they represent four diverse habits of the human eye. The deer hunter habitually watches the next bend; the duck hunter watches the skyline; the bird hunter watches the dog; the non-hunter does not watch."

Leopold spent his life tracking and watching deer, studying their behavior and thinking about them. After following countless deer trails around the shack, Leopold, wrote in his journal: "I have often noticed that a deer's taste in scenery and solitude is very much like my own."

Each March, Leopold studied the white pines near

In 1935, Leopold acquired an abandoned, worn-out shack near Baraboo, Wis., to serve as a base for deer hunts. "It is here," he wrote, "that we seek — and still find — our meat from God."

his shack along the Wisconsin River in Sauk County. The height of the browse lines told him the extent of the whitetail's hunger:

"A deer full of corn is too lazy to nip branches more than four feet above the ground; a really hungry deer rises on his hind legs and nips as high as eight feet."

Each October, Leopold returned to his pines to study the signs of the rut and record his findings in one of his shack sketches.

"A jack pine about eight feet high, and standing alone, seems especially to incite in a buck the idea that the world needs prodding. Such a tree must perforce turn the other cheek also, and emerges much the worse for wear. The only element of justice in such combats is that the more the tree is punished, the more pitch the buck carries away on his not-so shiny antlers."

Throughout his life, Leopold became more involved with deer than any other wildlife. He devoted his early career with the U.S. Forest Service in the Southwest to understanding deer ecology in the Gila and Kaibab national forests. His efforts in conservation focused on organizing sportsmen to protect deer and increase their numbers. When he moved to Madison, Wis., in 1924, he spent his time comparing the deer situation in the Northern Forest of the Great Lakes states with that in the Southwest.

In his final turbulent years as a Wisconsin conservation commissioner, he fought hunters who opposed reducing the deer herds.

"His assault on the citadel of the sacred doe, coming so soon after it was built and fortified, was an undertaking worthy of Indiana Jones," said deer biologist Dale McCullough.

Leopold even dreamed about deer. In an unpublished fragment titled "A Deerhunter's Dreams," he notes that every hunter dreams about the abundance of deer in the old days:

With the November sun on his back and the mountain breeze in his face, he threads his imaginary way down the juniper-scented ridges, Winchester rifle ready in hand, buckskin fringes softly tickling his wrist, his mind singing the deer-hunter's song —

   When the frost is on the pumpkin
   and the bucks are in the blue ...

His eager eye sees a possible rocking-chair head behind every bush. His straining ear hears something. He wakes up. It is the milk-wagon.

At his deer shack, Leopold grew in wisdom and knowledge as he studied the interrelationships between deer and plants, grasses, shrubs and trees. When deer are allowed to increase their numbers without increasing their natural food supply, calamity occurs to the timber, the flora, the birds and the deer. Restoring the damage inflicted by excess deer on forest plants can require 10 to 50 years. Leopold argued that responsible stewards could not allow the elimination of various plant species by deer overbrowsing their range. Instead, deer herds must be regulated and adjusted to land use. Deer hunting must be viewed as an instrument of control in maintaining a desirable relationship between deer populations, farming and forestry. We must think about deer and the land's integrity.

Leopold approved of regulated and disciplined deer hunting as a form of human behavior consistent with the land ethic. J. Baird Callicott, a professor of philosophy and a staunch defender of Leopold's land ethic, underscores Leopold's defense of deer hunting:

"To hunt and kill a white-tailed deer in certain districts may not only be ethically permissible, it might actually be a moral requirement, necessary to protect the local environment, taken as a whole, from the disintegrating effects of a cervid population explosion."

Leopold — who was influenced by cultural historian Frederick Jackson Turner, his neighbor on Van Hise Avenue in Madison — not only viewed deer hunting as an instrument of control, but as a re-enactment of our cultural past and re-creation of our pioneer heritage. Leopold held to the "one-bullet-one-buck" idea, and preferred primitive weapons without technological gadgetry. Like Turner and Theodore Roosevelt, Leopold believed that when man returns to primitive weapons to hunt, deer hunting preserves American virtues forged on the frontier. In this sense, deer hunting becomes not only morally ennobling but spiritually expansive.

Hunting for Aldo Leopold was a way of life, a way of being wild, but being bound by ethical restraints. Like William Faulkner, he viewed the deer hunt as an evolutionary challenge, a communion with the wild life of the prey, and an intimate bond with his deer

The image has a vertical caption on the right edge: University of Wisconsin-Madison Archives.

Leopold preparing a grouse for a deer camp meal.

hunting comrades. It fulfilled his own wild youth and reminded him of his dependency on the soil-plant-animal-man food chain. As a recreational deer hunter, Leopold enjoyed the hunt and achieved significant communion with nature. And yet, like Faulkner, he agonized over the paradox that his bond with nature appeared strongest only when he killed the object he loves — the white-tailed deer.

Regardless of location — whether in the Gila of New Mexico, the Sierra Madre of northern Mexico, or the "Sand County" of Wisconsin — the Leopold deer camp consisted of several basic ingredients:

(1) glee club singing of Spanish songs around the campfire; (2) enhanced by rounds of "cherry bounce," a special Leopold libation; (3) male bonding; (4) storytelling, what Faulkner called "the best of all breathing," galvanized by the drama and romance of shed deer blood; (5) exquisite venison cuisine; (6) re-enactment of cultural and natural history via the use of primitive weapons; (7) journal writing and recording every shot by target, date, distance, result and alibi, as well as

C.M. Russell Museum. Great Falls, Mont.

detailed information on weather conditions, other game seen, and animal behavior; and (8) a love for hunting deer on horseback while backpacking in wilderness areas.

One of the last deer hunts recorded in Leopold's journals occurred during the Christmas holidays of 1937-38. This was a pack-trip along the Rio Gavilan in the Chihuahua Sierra of northern Mexico. Leopold enjoyed deer hunting an area that retained the virgin stability of its soils, and the beauty and integrity of its flora and fauna. This 16-day hunt unfolded in the breaks of the Gavilan at "a beautiful campsite with many oaks for scenery and good wood," which was located at the foot of Chocolate Drop Hill. Leopold, his son Starker and brother Carl saw more than 250 deer while stalking them among ancient Indian ruins. Although the archers left empty-handed, Carl took two bucks and a doe with his Winchester. Their deer camp suppers consisted of turkey legs, quail and venison cutlets.

The scenery of the Gavilan campsite inspired Leopold to write his essay "Song of the Gavilan," in which he described one of his missed opportunities for a white-tailed buck. This eloquent passage is embedded with layers of cultural history that go deep into our past and deep into the future:

"One day, by aid of a roaring wind, I crept down upon a buck bedded on a dam. He lay in the shade of a great oak whose roots grasped the ancient masonry. His horns and ears were silhouetted against the golden grama beyond, in which grew the green rosette of mescal. The whole scene had the balance of a well-laid centerpiece. I overshot, my arrow splintering on the rocks the old Indian had laid. As the buck bounded down the mountain with a good-bye wave of his snowy flag, I realized that he and I were actors in an allegory. Dust to dust, stone age to stone age, but always the eternal chase! . . .

"Some day my buck will get a .30-30 in his glossy ribs."

Sunny Glade. **Oil on canvas. Charles M. Russell, 1913.**

FA
NOBL

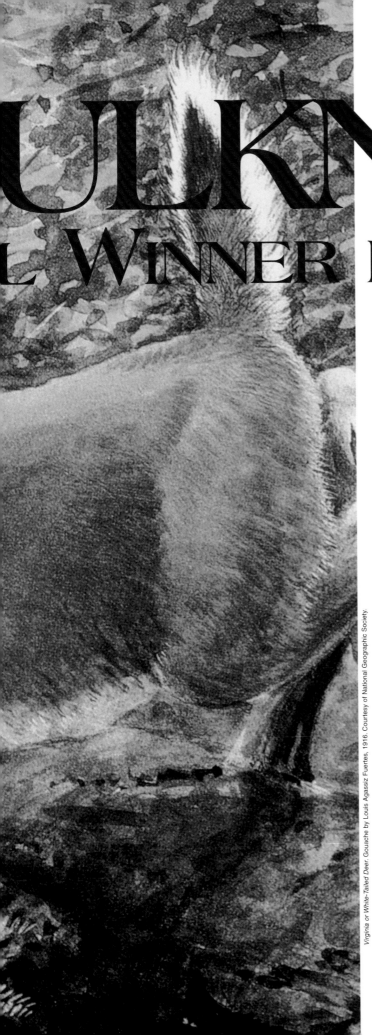

ULKNER
L WINNER IN CAMP

Virginia or White-Tailed Deer. Gouache by Louis Agassiz Fuertes, 1916. Courtesy of National Geographic Society.

"Then the buck was there. He did not come into sight; he was just there, looking not like a ghost but as if all of the light were condensed in him and he were the source of it, not only moving in it but disseminating it, already running, seen first as you always see the deer, in that split second after he has already seen you, already slanting away in that first soaring bound, the antlers even in that dim light looking like a small rocking-chair balanced on his head."

— William Faulkner,
"The Old People," *Harper's Monthly*,
September 1940.

Rob Wegner Photo Collection.

In 1909, a 12-year-old Mississippi deer hunter named William Faulkner (1897-1962) killed a white-tailed buck on the last gray day of the November deer hunt. The boy did not remember the shot, nor the recoil of the double-barreled shotgun, but with that shot the boy was initiated into deer hunting.

His mentor and guide, Sam Fathers, a Chickasaw Indian chief and quadroon slave, was well-versed in woodslore and whitetail wisdom. In a hunting baptismal rite, the guide "dipped his hands in the hot smoking blood and wiped them back and forth across the boy's face," Faulkner wrote in his story "The Old People," first published in *Harper's Monthly* in September 1940. Fathers not only initiated young Faulkner into deer hunting, he taught the boy the full range of the deer hunter's code, which was developed by such hunter-naturalists as George Shiras III and Theodore Roosevelt, and later enhanced by Aldo Leopold.

In "The Old People," Faulkner wrote that Fathers taught him "the woods, to hunt, when to shoot and when not to shoot, when to kill and when not to kill, and better, what to do with it afterward." This deer hunting story reveals the initiation of a boy (first called "I" referring to Faulkner himself, and in its later version Isaac "Ike" McCaslin) into the life of a deer hunter, into manhood and ultimately into the metaphysical mysteries of hunting the big woods in the Mississippi Delta, a land Faulkner immortalized. Faulkner imbues this tale with a mythic atmosphere bordering on the religious and supernatural. The story opens in a Genesis-like way that invokes biblical language of the world's creation:

"At first there was nothing. There was the faint, cold, steady rain, the gray and constant light of the late November dawn, with the voices of the hounds converging somewhere in it and toward them."

This passage contains a Wagnerian sense of anticipation and awe the boy experiences when first seeing the phantom white-tailed buck — the great buck many hunters believed did not cast an actual shadow, although it made tracks and cast antlers, big tracks and big antlers!

Faulkner describes a scene of the boy taking his position to wait for the legendary buck:

"Then, as if it had waited for them to find their positions and become still, the wilderness breathed again. It seemed to lean inward above them, above himself and Sam and Walter and Boon in their separate lurking-places, tremendous, attentive, impartial and omniscient, the buck moving in it somewhere."

This ghost buck would disappear the first day of the deer season only to reappear the day after the season closed. This buck disappeared as mysteriously as it emerged, like a sharply focused slide projected on a screen slowly blurring until vanishing into what Faulkner called "dappled obscurity." The boy's first sighting of the great buck, the symbol of the wilderness's spirit, represents an experience of the supernatural in which the identity of the hunter and hunted become one.

In Faulkner's "Big Woods," we find the whitetail in a wilderness of revelation, which allows the

Faulkner in his library sanctuary at Rowan Oak with his cherished Underwood portable. He actually composed in longhand. "I've got to feel the pencil and see the words at the end of the pencil," he said.

Rob Wegner Photo Collection.

A deer hunting postcard of the time.

deer hunter to see the divine unencumbered by the everyday realities of civilization. Nowhere in the history of American literature do we get a greater sense of the reverence, awe and anticipation involved when the young hunter encounters the legendary white-tailed buck of mythic proportion:

"Then the boy saw the buck. It was coming down the ridge, as if it were walking out of the very sound of the (hunting) horn which related its death. It was not running, it was walking, tremendous, unhurried, slanting and tilting it head to pass the antlers through the undergrowth. ...

"Then it saw them. And still it did not begin to run. It just stopped for an instant, taller than any man, looking at them; then its muscles suppled, gathered. It did not even alter its course, not fleeing, not even running, just moving with that winged and effortless ease with which deer move, passing within twenty feet of them, its head high and the eyes not proud and not haughty but just full and wild and unafraid."

For Faulkner, the ghost-buck takes on a life of its own, one with transcendent qualities, often becoming "unkillable," remaining forever at large despite overwhelming odds against it. This situation explains why buck hunting became such a passion for William Faulkner, and why it became a way of life, not just a hobby. In his *Southern Hunting in Black and White* (1991), Stuart Marks, an independent scholar, underscores the passion for buck hunting by emphasizing "most bucks remain at large, unrestrained by property lines, and free to roam the minds of men who are themselves restrained. For most buck hunters, these large creatures remain beyond their grasp and, through time, come to symbolize the ones that always get away."

This particular buck, however, did not get away. With its death and the spilling of its blood, the boy was initiated into the mysteries of the whitetail and the glorification of the wilderness by Sam Fathers, shaman of deer forests, high priest of nature, and guru of deer camp. This spiritual guide, an embodiment of nature's noble qualities, not only taught the young neophyte how to kill deer, but how to live comfortably in the woods. Faulkner learned to know the deer's social behavior; to travel with the aid of the stars, a compass and tree markings; and to patiently stay in a deer stand for hours — watching, listening, waiting and observing. Fathers tutored the boy on a way of life that centers around hunting, a philosophy of living that meshes with the cult of the whitetail. Fathers also shared his own Chickasaw heritage with its deep respect for whitetailed deer.

Sam Fathers showed the boy the difference between tracks made by bucks and does, and explained the different sounds the two sexes make while moving through the woods. Fathers instructed the boy to shed all instruments of civilization so he would be granted a closer view of this magnificent animal. Even after entering the whitetail's sacred space, it is not until the boy surrenders his knife, compass and gun and becomes lost and unarmed in the buck's bailiwick that he suddenly stands in the phantom buck's mysterious presence.

Fathers and the boy often pursued the buck without weapons, without intent of shooting. By doing so, they found the animal tolerated their approach, allowing them to intimately learn the deer's social behavior and defense mechanisms. Following his Chickasaw heritage, Fathers taught the neophyte to live in simplicity, purity and close communion with the whitetail — to eat its flesh and wear its skin; to become one with the spirit of the deer; to recognize the animal as a real, living entity with spiritual substance. As a result, the boy became a natural gentleman and master deer hunter who learned to shoot deer with certainty, respect and reverence.

For Faulkner's deer hunting clan, the whitetail became mysterious, and extraordinarily large and competent. Hunters, Fathers argued, must see whitetails in supernatural terms and as the embodiment of large principles and ethical concepts. Because of these spiritual teachings, the boy

A Mississippi Delta deer camp scene, 1897. The photo was taken by Dr. N. Yeates at the Boyce Lake Hunting Camp near Lambert, Miss. A female deer hunter appears at the far left.

Mississippi Department of Archives and History.

remained devoted to the November deer hunt the rest of his life.

In "Devout Observances," Chapter 12 of his book on economic thought, *The Theory of the Leisure Class* (1899), Thorstein Veblen made formal the idea of a close relationship between the deer hunting temperament and sacred reverence. He wrote that the recreation of deer hunting "has some efficacy as a means of grace ... that its activities come to do duty as a novitiate or a means of induction into that fuller unfolding of the life of spiritual status." This book remained on Faulkner's list of recommended readings.

Today's advocate of this idea is Holmes Rolston III, a professor of philosophy at Colorado State University. He argues in his *Environmental Ethics* (1988), that "hunting is not sport; it is a sacrament of the fundamental, mandatory seeking and taking possession of value that characterizes an ecosystem and from which no culture ever escapes ... Hunting, a seeming sport, has sacramental value because it unfolds the contradictions of the universe."

Deer hunting takes us beyond mere observation, and makes us direct participants in nature. It educates us about the natural world and returns us to our blood and origins. When we draw blood, kill a whitetail and eat its venison in an earthy way, we educate ourselves in the philosophy of ecology. Nobel laureate William Faulkner believed in that idea, as did ecologist Aldo Leopold, and both lived that idea to its fullest extent at their deer camps.

As Faulkner wrote, drawing "honorable blood worthy of being drawn" represents the culminating point of the November deer hunt. Unlike Ernest Hemingway, Faulkner did not emphasize the pleasure of killing. Instead, he valued the symbolic importance of the act and the pleasure of pursuit. Faulkner's deer hunting stories need to be read and reread in deer camp. Earned self-respect — not esteem in the eyes of other hunters — and the savory taste of venison tenderloins constitute the deer hunter's ultimate reward. As long as the challenge exists, as long as the white-tailed buck runs in the deer woods, life is worth living and deer hunting worthy of the effort.

When the boy learns the main joy of deer hunting lies in the pursuit, and that the pleasure of the hunt develops from anticipation and the chase itself — not the alleged goal — the boy completes his education in the Big Woods of the Mississippi Delta. Sam Fathers is his mentor, the Big Woods where the buck roams is his college, and the legendary white-tailed buck is his course book.

When the boy kills his first buck on that gray, rainy day in November 1909, he confronts the hunter's paradox: How can man kill the object he loves? This paradox is an underlying theme in Faulkner's hunting stories.

In "The Old People," Faulkner wrote: "Because he was just twelve then, that morning something had happened to him: in less than a second he has ceased forever to be the child he was yesterday. Or perhaps that made no difference, perhaps even a city-bred man, let alone a child, could not have understood it; perhaps only a country-bred one

White-Tailed Deer — Aristocrat of American Game.
Francis Lee Jacques, 1943. Oil on canvas. Rob Wegner
Photo Collection.

Courtesy of Larry Zach.

could comprehend loving the life he spills. He began to shake again."

Faulkner was a country-bred man who was an accomplished hunter by age 12 because of his father's passion for hunting deer. The boy received an air rifle at age 6, a .22 rifle at age 8, a .410 shotgun at age 10, and a 12-gauge shotgun at age 12. At each stage, he was taught how to use them for hunting. He eventually received the highly cherished Winchester .30-30 Model '94 deer rifle.

In his essay, "Do You Write, Mr. Faulkner?," Ron Rash notes that Faulkner was "destined to be a hunter and outdoorsman, for patience, self-discipline, and an ability to work in solitude, the traits of both writer and outdoorsman, marked his character and temperament. These traits developed amidst a family and a society that made his interest in hunting and the outdoors almost inevitable."

According to his brother John, William Faulkner liked to talk about deer and deer hunting as much as hunting the deer itself. When asked by an interviewer how far back deer hunting went in his family, John Faulkner said, "*Falconer* — which means hunter — was the spelling of our family name in England, and this goes back to the 1600s."

As with his great-grandfather, William Clark Faulkner, known as "The Old Colonel," William Faulkner was wedded to deer hunting's mythology to the point of obsession. He was always determined to be the man with the rifle, the one who rode horses while hunting with great gusto. Like Theodore Roosevelt, he loved nothing more than to ride, jump and chase animals on horseback to the music of bugled-voiced hounds. When he rode, he wore his favorite hunt jacket, which was lovingly patched and repatched at the elbows.

If you want to understand the ritual of deer hunting, you must read Faulkner's hunting stories. In his life and writings, Faulkner never forgot that first kill. That scene and its ethical importance continually returned to his memories and writings. He relived it again in "Delta Autumn," an article first

For Faulkner's deer hunting group, the whitetail became larger than life, as illustrated in this Larry Zach painting of the Russ Clarken nontypical buck.

published in *Story* magazine and later in the novel *Go Down, Moses* (1942), a Bildungsroman in which deer hunting plays a crucial role in the central character's development:

"Sam dipped his hands into the hot blood and marked his face forever while he stood trying not to tremble, humbly and with pride too though the boy of twelve had been unable to phrase it then: I slew you; my bearing must not shame your quitting life. My conduct forever onward must become your death."

Rob Wegner Photo Collection.

The boy's conduct must not shame the whitetail's death. In Faulkner's case, it never did. He transferred to a broader realm of human existence an ethical code he inherited, developed and assimilated into his deer hunting experiences. That ethical code consisted of humility when confronting the whitetail on its terms, and pride in developing hunting skills and loyalty to his deer hunting companions. In *Old Times in the Faulkner Country* (1975) John Cullen — a practical joker, backwoods humorist and one of Faulkner's deer hunting companions — reported that "Faulkner proved himself to be a good hunter and one of the fairest and most agreeable men we ever had in our deer camp."

Faulkner hunted at General James Stone's deer camp in the Delta. This camp was located near Anguilla, due west of Yazoo City and almost in the corner where Mississippi, Louisiana and Arkansas meet. In Stone's camp — which was founded short-

Left, the comical side of deer camp. Circa 1930. Below, a Mississippi Delta camp on Low Copperas Bayou, Dec. 26,1900.

Mississippi Department of Archives and History.

Camp on Low Copperas Bayou
Tallahatchie Co - Miss - Dec 26-1900

Rob Wegner Photo Collection.

A deer hunting postcard — the epitome of North American deer camp mystique.

ly after the Civil War — judges, lawyers and bankers hunted with men paid by the hour, and all shared equally in deer camp duties. When there, Faulkner donned a burlap sack as apron and cleaned pots, pans and dirty dishes in a tub.

This deer camp was also near Cypress Lake and the Big Sunflower River, an area now marked by the Delta National Forest to the south and the Yazoo National Wildlife Refuge to the north. Faulkner often slept outdoors under the stars in his sleeping bag. For meals, he indulged in his favorite food: coon and collards. According to a deer hunting buddy, he even ate coon and collards for breakfast.

In his life and in his fiction, Faulkner cherished deer camp in the Big Woods of the Delta. Deer camp stood as a holy place where hunters experienced self-renewal, spiritual communion and a sense of brotherhood. Deer camp was a major social event, a manly, democratic affair — a great social equalizer — played out in a 100-year-old setting. Faulkner believed deer hunters were not white, black or red. Rather, they were "men, hunters, with the will and hardihood to endure and the humility and skill to survive."

A galvanized tin shack eventually served as the focal point for this annual retreat. Here, Faulkner and his hunting partners assembled each autumn to hunt whitetails, commune with nature, tell tall tales, play poker, eat venison and participate in masculine camaraderie at the campfire. Stephen Oates, one of Faulkner's biographers, wrote: "Faulkner was a regular member of this ritualistic annual retreat. ... He enjoyed the evening of drinking and tale telling, the huntsmen's laughing silhouettes in the glare of the campfire. He liked to stalk deer, to pit himself against the cunning of the wild animal. But beyond that, he felt a sacred kinship with the Big Woods, which allowed him a temporary refuge from the corruptions of civilization. Out here a man could remember his values — his honor and pride and independence — which alone made him worth saving but which civilization threatened with its dehumanizing technology, its onerous government controls and handouts."

After creating its charter, Faulkner eventually

incorporated this deer camp into the Okatoba Hunting and Fishing Club and served as its president. In his book, *My Brother Bill: An Affectionate Reminiscence* (1963), Faulkner's brother John boasted that Bill served his apprenticeship well and "was blooded" for his first buck. Before his hunting days were over, John recalled, William became one of the grand old men of the deer camp and served as its captain.

Faulkner's deer camp, located on the Sunflower River in the heart of the Delta in Sharkey County, stimulated much of his best writing. It meant many things to "Mr. Bill," as his comrades fondly called him. He enjoyed not only the mystical sweet sound of hunting horns and baying deer hounds, but also the escapism, wood smoke, male bonding, achieving of self-identity, returning to primitive life, the aromatic smell of venison in the pot, a utilitarian quest for venison and, ultimately, the magical meeting of wilderness and whiskey in the forest's quietude.

Hunting historian Thomas Altherr observes that "the stimulation of ever present alcohol added a feeling of homeopathic magic to the scene and a ritual salute to the beast."

Faulkner describes whiskey drinking as a form of communion and an ultimate salute to the quarry. He did not view it as an attempt to acquire virtues of courage or cunning, but rather to honor these attributes:

"There was always a bottle present, so that it would seem to (the boy) that those fine fierce instants of heart and brain and courage and wiliness and speed were concentrated and distilled into the brown liquor which not women, not boys and children, but only hunters drank, drinking not of the blood they spilled but some condensation of the wild immortal spirit, drinking it moderately, humbly even, not with pagan's base and baseless hope of acquiring the virtues of cunning and strength and speed but in the salute to them."

The fact that Faulkner's camp reportedly once debated the possibility of catching a buck with a hula hoop leads one to think "drinking it moderately," as Faulkner maintained, might have been exceeded occasionally. For instance, Faulkner's deer camp crony John Cullen, a concrete worker, reports they "took a little nip of antifreeze every now and then."

During the 1930s and '40s, Faulkner spent a great deal of time in deer camp. The Delta became a sanctuary from his anxieties. Whitetails, however, were scarce. In 1929, Leopold reported in his *Game*

Hard to Beat   'Four of a Kind.

Rob Wegner Photo Collection.

This postcard shows that deer and bear were still abundant in 1906 in the Mississippi Delta.

Survey that only small herds remained in limited parts of the Delta. But in 1932, sportsmen helped establish the Mississippi Game and Fish Commission. By the 1940s, a deer restoration project, funded basically by Pittman-Robertson money, was under way. Translocated whitetails from Texas, Mexico and North Carolina began to appear near the cherished tin hut.

This galvanized tin structure, surrounded by jeeps and pickups, served as a man's world. Sixteen bunks circled the shack's walls, except for a kitchen at one end. One luxury prevailed: electricity. It allowed a refrigerator to cool the beer and venison Faulkner and his friends often ate for breakfast.

In his characterization of Ike McCaslin, Faulkner portrays the American buck hunter in the typical, masculine, Southern tradition. As Stuart Marks

State Historical Society of Wisconsin.

The eternal deer camp scene: sitting before the burning fire with whiskey in hand. Circa 1940s.

wrote, the buck hunter is "the epitome of a masculine mystique. He is cool and collected in the trying and risky moments of performance. He uses his mind instead of his emotion in situations where discretion is essential before action. He is active and assertive in the appropriate context and shows control in any situation likely to compromise him. He knows how to win appropriately, and does not cause others to become jealous or envious of his triumphs."

Faulkner's deer camp partners had not read his writing. As one astute observer described it, they were "natural beyond all sophistication." Just how natural is evident in farmer Bob Evans' comments about Faulkner in the documentary film *William Faulkner: A Life on Paper* (1980), produced by the Mississippi Center for Educational Television. Evans said: "Bill Faulkner was a fine, fine hunter; he was a quiet hunter. Fact of the business, he was a pretty quiet man in camp. You didn't never hear no hooraying and storming and all this, that, and the other going on from Bill. Now, he would laugh and talk and tell little stories."

In deer camp, this world-renowned author never mentioned his books or anything about writing. He remained a good ol' boy who hunted with his cronies and never mentioned his calling or success. While others played poker, the great American author sipped Jack Daniels by the campfire while smoking his pipe. He listened more than talked, and spent a lot of time planning the next day's deer hunt in the Delta's canebrakes, thickets and jungles. His biographer, Joseph Blotner, characterized deer camp in his two-volume biography, *Faulkner: A Biography* (1991):

"At first, they would eat pork, but before a full day passed, old Ad Bush would be cooking squirrel and coon. They would go out in the four-o-clock darkness, making their way through the thick brush into the deer woods, the leashed dogs sniffing and barking. Then the drive would begin, the hunters poised at their stands for the dash of the buck. At the end of the long day they would sit around the campfire drinking whiskey, waiting to eat the plain, hearty fare at the rough-hewn table. After clean-up chores, the storytelling and the nickel poker would while away the short evenings. Faulkner enjoyed it, hardly distinguishable from the others in his stained hunting clothes and worn slouch hat. He told some of the memorable tales, but most of the time he would listen, and often he would sit reading a book."

Faulkner's ultimate devotion to deer and the annual November hunt showed itself in his response to the Nobel Prize for literature. On Nov. 10, 1950, he received a phone call at his "Rowan Oak" residence from a Swedish journalist, who informed him he had won the 1949 Nobel Prize for literature. When the journalist asked whether he would come to Sweden to receive the prize, Faulkner said: "I can't get away. I'm going deer hunting!" His family then struggled to get him to take the call from Sweden that would make the announcement official! After receiving the call, Faulkner informed the Nobel Prize officials by mail that he would not be present at the ceremony. The next day he packed his guns and gear, and left for a week in deer camp.

Faulkner's deer camp now housed a Nobel Prize winner. He said nothing to his hunting companions, but they soon learned of the feat from a newspaper someone brought to camp. That night, they celebrated with one of Faulkner's favorite meals: coon and collards simmered in a cast-iron pot by "Uncle Ike" Roberts, an old friend and hunting crony. Roberts — who was also a former sheriff of Oxford and the dean of Faulkner's deer hunting crowd — was often referred to as "camp boss."

While Faulkner scrubbed dishes that night, Uncle Ike asked Mr. Bill what he would do if the Swedish ambassador came to camp and handed him the money. Faulkner replied: "I'd tell him to put it on the table and grab a drying rag and pitch in!" Delighted with his response, everyone took a nightcap or two of "Old Crow." Actually, the nightcaps lasted until 3 a.m.

Faulkner eventually went to Sweden to accept the Nobel Prize. When he returned, he encountered Uncle Ike at the Oxford courthouse. The following dialogue was recorded in a documentary film by the Ford Foundation. It originally aired on CBS's Omnibus in December 1952:

Uncle Ike: "Where you been?"

Faulkner: "Sweden."

Uncle Ike: "You got the prize I hear. That's good. (Pause) Long time to deer season. Month or two anyway."

Faulkner: "We'll get us a big one this year, you watch."

As Faulkner departs, Uncle Ike turns to the camera and says: "Bill Faulkner is a full hand at anything he does. The rule is, that the deer hunter stays on the stand from sunup until he hears the three long blows on the horn from the man who is following the dogs. Bill will stay on the stand until after sundown if he doesn't hear the horn. Someone will have to go by and get him. He'll pick up the smutty end of a log as quick as anyone when the fire needs attention."

After Faulkner returned from Sweden, one of his deer camp cronies, John Cullen, sent King Gustav VI of Sweden this message:

Faulkner during the late 1930s. At this time, he was writing deer hunting stories based on his adventures in the Mississippi Delta.

Marshall Smith. Courtesy of the William Boozer Collection.

Oxford, Mississippi
December 13, 1950
King Gustav VI of Sweden
Stockholm, Sweden

Your Majesty:

I saw a picture of you giving William Faulkner a prize last Monday, and I'll bet William didn't tell you what a big coon and collards eater he is. Now, I told William to carry some delicious coon and collards to you. If he had, I am sure you would have given him a larger prize. In spite of William's dereliction in this respect, I am sure you like him, because he is the kindest and most courteous person I ever knew. Knowing this, I am sure he treated you with royal respect and courtesy.

I want to tell you a little secret, though, about William. He is sometimes incorrigible; he doesn't do everything I tell him to do. Proof of this was found on our recent deer hunt when I was head dishwasher. (Incidentally, this mastery of mine over William on that occasion convinces me that oftentimes I am greater than he is.) William disobeyed me then; he wanted to get the dishes cleaner than I did, and took too much time at that job. It is said, although I don't believe it, that William volunteered for this chore because he did not want to eat from the dishes I washed. His dis-obedience did not provoke me to action, although I am twice as large as William, for I remembered that when we were boys we never jumped on anybody his size but always picked out a man-mountain.

Since you have been so nice to our friend, Mr. Ike Roberts and I and all the rest of the boys invite you to our camp next Fall for a coon and collard dinner, for if you are a friend of William Faulkner's you are a friend of ours. This *includes the cooks, the horses and the hounds.*

His Majesty proved to be a good sport and graciously accepted the joke:

Stockholm
December 23, 1950
Mr. John Cullen
Oxford, Mississippi

Dear Mr. Cullen,
H. M. the King of Sweden has read your letter about Mr. Faulkner with great pleasure. As His Majesty does not ride nor shoot, I am afraid he will not enjoy your planned deer hunting party in Mississippi, but sends you nevertheless His thanks for your kind thought and His best wishes for the new year.
Yours faithfully,
Erik Sjoqvist
His Majesty's Private Secretary

Cullen sincerely regretted the king declining the invitation, but quickly admitted that, "although we sincerely regretted that the King could not come, I guess it was just as well that he did not. It is doubtful that I could have taught some of the members of our camp the proper etiquette for associating with his Majesty. Despite all I could have told them, some of them might have been calling him Gussie before the hunt was over, such as Big Red Brite."

In addition to Uncle Ike Roberts and John Cullen, Faulkner's deer-camp crowd consisted of Dr. Felix Linder, a physician and boyhood friend; Uncle Bud Miller ("Walton"), a highway worker; Leo Calloway, Faulkner's old school seatmate; Uncle Bob Evans, "a dry-wit ham-handed farmer"; Bob Harkins, a ginner and miller; and Big Red Brite, a store clerk and a total abstainer. Red Brite has been characterized as a mountain of a man, relaxed, friendly and good-natured. In a tape-recorded interview, he described Faulkner this way:

"Bill Faulkner was the best hunter there was. I'd say he was as good as they come. He was a good shot and true — what you'd call a true-blue hunter, I'll tell you that.

"But talk about him shooting: I've seen him take that .30-30 Winchester rifle and shoot turtles off of logs while he was going down the Sunflower River in the motorboat.

"Bill would stay through thick and thin; if it was muddy he was there, or if it was dry he was there. That's what we ... called a true-blue hunter."

Faulkner believed noble qualities can be learned from a life nurtured by nature: truth and honor, pride and endurance. Faulkner insisted that many of man's most admirable traits — courage, responsibility, independence and compassion — are best learned in the woods and deer camp. Like Aldo Leopold, Faulkner saw deer hunting as a legitimate form of nature and part of one's education. Leopold even argued that deer hunting provides a hunter with a liberal education.

Sam Fathers taught the boy the qualities that best sum up the deer hunter's code as Faulkner developed it: strength, endurance, bravery, honor, dignity, pride, humility, pity, and love of liberty and justice. He enforced these virtues with three basic insights: a knowledge of death, a deep sense of the sublime, and a profound awareness of mystic unity. He linked the very sight of a whitetail to a spiritual unity between man and deer. The ultimate value of this deer hunting ethic derives from the timelessness of the ritual, and its dramatic power to spiritually bind events and people engaged in rigorous activity. Faulkner wrote:

"The wilderness watched them pass, less than inimical now and never to be inimical again since the buck still and forever leaped, the shaking gun barrels coming constantly and forever steady at last, crashing, and still out of his instant of immortality the buck sprang, forever immortal; — the wagon jolting and bouncing on, the movement of the buck, the shot, Sam Fathers and himself and the blood with which Sam had marked him forever one with the wilderness which had accepted him since Sam said that he had done all right."

The buck's "instant of immortality," as Faulkner calls it, becomes the hunter's. The deer hunter is no longer hostile to the woods. The woods accepts the hunter. When he leaves the wilderness, it goes with him. He knows it will forever be a home that will accept him when he returns. The white-tailed buck, "forever immortal" represents a symbol for the hunter of everything he gains from the wilderness experience.

As Daniel Hoffman argues in *Faulkner's Country Matters* (1989), "The huge buck is both a real beast and a totem, to be seen only by the spiritually worthy." The deer woods becomes the cathedral of the mind in which the hunter sees timelessness coexisting with the temporal world of deer hunting. At this point, the hunter understands his organic connection with mounted bucks on the study wall. The white-tailed deer becomes the epitome and glorification of all wildlife.

As Faulkner approached age 60, the fire and passion for pursuing deer began to mellow. In a letter written shortly before the November 1954 deer hunt, he wrote: "No, I shan't shoot a deer. I don't want to shoot deer, just pursue them on a horse." In another letter to a friend he mentioned he had missed a 12-pointer the previous season:

"He was a beautiful creature, broke out of a thicket 100 yards away running like a horse, perfectly flat, not jumping at all, doing about 30 miles per hour, ran in full view for 75 yards, I picked two perfect openings in trees and shot twice. I left my customary .30-30 Winchester carbine at home for my boy to use and was shooting a .270 bolt-action. I think the first bullet hit a twig and blew up. The second one missed him clear, over or maybe behind him; he was just running too fast. He was a beautiful sight. I'm glad now he got away from me though I would have liked his head."

In "Race at Morning," one of the four great hunting stories in *Big Woods*, the major event — the shooting of a white-tailed buck — becomes a non-event. After tracking a big buck for several years, the boy narrator and a fellow named Mr. Ernest let the buck go. Afterward, Mr. Ernest asks the boy some questions:

"Which would you rather have? His bloody head

and hide on the kitchen floor yonder and half his meat in a pickup truck on the way to Yoknapatawpha County, or him with his head and hide and meat still together over yonder in that brake, waiting for next November for us to run him again?"

When asked in a university interview why he hunted, Faulkner responded: "always to learn something, to learn something of — not only to pursue but to overtake and then to have compas-

Courtesy of Larry Zach.

Broken Solitude — Whitetail. **Painting by Larry Zach.**

sion not to destroy, to catch, to touch, and then let go because then tomorrow you can pursue again. If you destroy it, what you caught, then it's gone, it's finished. And that to me is sometimes the greater part of valor but always it's the greater part of pleasure, not to destroy what you have pursued. The pursuit is the thing, not the reward, not the gain."

In Faulkner's world, the boy learns from the hunters' talk that two kinds of hunting exist: hunting to kill and hunting to hunt. Hunting to hunt,

that is, keeping the yearly rendezvous with the animal, often remained supreme for Faulkner. That activity entails getting the legendary buck in your sights and then letting him go — sacredly witnessing the whitetail but not shooting.

Obviously, "Let 'Em Go, Let 'Em Grow," the banner of today's Quality Deer Management Association, is hardly a new idea. Watching the

Courtesy of Brett Smith.

great buck with reverence, but not shooting, and thus becoming an initiate of deeper mysteries, were ideas well-ingrained in the minds of Faulkner and Leopold during the 1930s and '40s. These men agreed that a deer hunter's awed response to the first buck sighting might be so overwhelming that it precludes the possibility of shooting. In *Go Down, Moses*, Sam Fathers sees an impressive buck and salutes him, crying, "Oleh, Chief Grandfather." In paying this awe-inspired American Indian tribute to the buck, Fathers demonstrates that such reverence for the noble animal can overcome the will to shoot, even for the most dedicated deer hunter.

Like Leopold, Faulkner viewed quality deer hunting as a serious matter to which a hunter dedicates his life. He defined it as a fundamental form of mythic activity in which man enters a spiritual bond with the deer and a social bond with his fellow man. Deer hunting for Leopold and Faulkner became not only a maturation process, but a return to primitive life, a yearly pageant-rite and an exercise in male bonding.

Frederick Karl portrays that bond in his book *William Faulkner: American Writer* (1989):

"This involved living under uncomfortable circumstances, eating a diet of game (or coon), staying damp most of the time, drinking ... after the day's hunt, rising early into chill and wet, standing still for several hours at a deer stand, occasionally getting a shot, but more often than not seeing nothing ... The Big Woods experience whatever its discomforts, was like renewal — not only for a complicated man like Faulkner but for other hunters, whose own feelings were allayed by this temporary life within a life. But it was not only the hunt; it was the anticipation that preceded it, and then the stories which evolved afterwards around the campsite ... Once the day had closed, dark has settled in, the fire has been lit, food is being prepared, whiskey is available — when that setting is created ... the stories can flow; and Faulkner had learned from and contributed to this process. ... The beauty of it was that it occurred outside civilization — it was as though the men had found an island separated by moat and drawbridge from everyone else. No wives, children, girlfriends, no debits and credits — the men established the terms on which they would be invited back, and that was all. Rifle in hand, they had each other — and it was a profound need in Faulkner to know he was welcome on these annual trips."

Faulkner's annual deer hunts in the Delta become collective ceremonial hunts, on the one hand, and individual initiations on the other: public ceremony and private revelation. But above all, they contain the witnessing in the wilderness of a sacred experience. When Ike sees the phantom buck, the moment is filled with quasi-religious meaning; the buck appears as if by magic

— the experience becomes a mystical encounter with the sacred. After SEEING the great buck — the spirit of the wilderness — Ike exclaims: "But I saw it! I saw him!" Seeing the shadowy buck in this timeless way, and bearing witness in this dramatic fashion, takes the deer hunting ritual to its highest plane.

In his book *Sport and the Spirit of Play in American Fiction* (1981), Christian Messenger, an English professor at the University of Illinois, notes that "the 'it' for Ike is nothing less than the majestic wilderness itself, which is the sum of all the lives that had passed away while it remained inviolate; the 'him' is cast as the buck himself, personification of the spirit of that timeless freedom. ... The ceremonial kill, the hunter as initiate, and the solitary witnessing in the wilderness are all part of the hunt, a hybrid sport which retains archaic elements of sacredness in dynamic fashion."

In this atmosphere, the hunter finds himself in an altered universe that approaches sacred mythology and mystery, and requires initiation rites. Faulkner's deer hunting stories, historian Thomas Altheer observed, contain "all the elements of an archetypal hunting initiation: the eager supplicant, the wilderness-wise primitive priest, the sacrificial prey, and a quasi-magical environment."

It seems likely Faulkner read the writings of Frank G. Speck (1881-1950), the leading anthropologist of his day, who made these comments on deer hunting in two papers published in *Bird-Lore and Frontiers* in 1938 and 1939:

"Deer hunting is not a war upon the animals, not a slaughter for food or profit, but a holy occupation. ...

"The hunter's virtue lies in respecting the soul of the animals killed, in treating their remains in a prescribed manner and in particular, in making use of as much of the carcass as possible. These observances constitute religious obedience. The animals slain under the proper conditions and treated with the consideration due them return to life again and again. They furthermore indicate their whereabouts to the 'good' hunter in dreams resigning themselves to his weapons in a free spirit of self-sacrifice."

Faulkner not only considered deer hunting a holy occupation, but a proper mode of environmental perception. As with James Fenimore Cooper, he believed the hunter acquires high levels of knowledge about nature — achieved beyond the kill and often acquired at the expense of the kill — and heightened spirituality. He defined deer hunting as "the best game of all, the best of all breathing and forever the best of all listening."

Unless you read Faulkner's deer hunting stories, you miss the best writing on the subject and the essence of what deer hunting is all about in a spiritual sense. Steeped in the hunting mythology of Sir James George Frazer's *The Golden Bough* (1922),

Courtesy of Brett Smith.

Phil Mullen. Courtesy of Cofield's Studio.

and the hair-splitting deer hunting tales of William Elliott — as found in his *Carolina Sports by Land and Water* (1846) — Faulkner's deer hunting narratives rank as the finest in the English language. Faulkner understood the white-tailed deer hunt and its metaphysical meaning better than anyone. He believed man hunts deer not for the kill or the blood, but for the skill and artistry involved in the chase. This belief manifests itself in his annual pilgrimages to his cherished tin hut in the Mississippi Delta. So traditional was this ritual handed down through the generations that it became known as "The Hunt."

According to the Oxford *Eagle*, Faulkner bagged a buck on "The Hunt" of 1949. In the January 1950 issue of *Mississippi Game and Fish*, deer biologists estimated Mississippi's deer kill for the 1949 deer season was 2,500. Sharkey County, where Faulkner and his boys — known as the "Legendary Oxford

Faulkner with some of his deer hunting friends. From left: "Red" Brite, John Cullen (back to camera), Faulkner, Ike Roberts (deer camp boss) and Bill Evans.

Deerslayers" — hunted, headed the list of counties with a harvest of 105. They also reported that Randolph Kuriger, from the famous McGraw's Deer Camp, shot the largest buck in the Delta that year near Lake George, an 11-pointer weighing 385 pounds. Sharkey County also led the state that year in the number of established deer camps, or those with a certificate of registration.

On Oct. 14, 1955, Random House published Faulkner's hunting stories in a volume titled *Big Woods*. It sold for $3.95, and went out of print after four printings. Today it sells for about $150 in the out-of-print book market. In 1988, The Limited Editions Club published two of the hunting stories from *Big Woods*, "The

Old People" and "The Bear" in a deluxe edition limited to 850 copies.

(I recently purchased a mint copy of this scarce, deluxe edition from Angler's & Shooter's Bookshelf for $450. It contains an introduction by Cleanth Brooks, a Yale University professor and noted Faulkner scholar, and etchings by Neil Welliver, a landscape painter and print maker. This edition is one of the most cherished volumes in my library of more than 2,000 volumes on deer and deer hunting.)

Welliver's etching of the great, phantom buck captures the ghostlike appearance of the whitetail as depicted in Faulkner's prose. In his introduction, professor Brooks notes these hunting stories were written by a man who loved the wilderness and the whitetails that live there. Indeed, Faulkner gives life to deer-hunting. Consider the young boy's first bout with buck fever:

"He stopped breathing then; there was only his heart, his blood, and in the following silence the wilderness ceased to breathe also, leaning, stooping overhead with its breath held, tremendous and impartial and waiting. Then the shaking stopped too, as he had known it would, and he drew back the two heavy hammers of the gun."

Although not considered one of Faulkner's major works by some literary critics, the book nevertheless received attention at the time by reviewers in newspapers, magazines and journals.

In May 1994, almost 40 years later, Vintage International reprinted Faulkner's *Big Woods* in an inexpensive paperback edition that was still in print in 2001.

Historically, storytelling begins with Stone Age hunters sitting around the campfire recounting their adventures. In writing about his deer hunting adventures from 1915 to 1950, Faulkner keeps that tradition alive. He was a great listener in his historic deer camp. Many of his hunting stories originated from campfires in the Big Woods. They are vividly real, yet mythological, universal and timeless. The endless reminiscing and talking of the "Oxford Legendary Deer Hunters" in front of the campfire on the Sunflower River underscored deer hunting's dignity for Faulkner:

"The voices quiet and weighty and deliberate for retrospection and recollection and exactitude among the concrete trophies — the racked guns and the heads and skins — in the libraries of town houses or the offices of plantation houses or (best of all) in the camps themselves where the intact and still-warm meat yet hung, the men who had slain it sitting before the burning logs on hearths when there were houses and hearths or about the smoky blazing of piled wood in front of stretched tarpaulins when there were not."

In these stories, Faulkner uses a language of vision and sacrament, a language filled with apparitions, ghostlike reality, superstitious faith, excited wonderment, and a heightened feeling for the phenomenal and the miraculous — all bordering on the hallucinatory. The deer hunter comes home in these stories. He returns to a lost homeland. The sighting of the whitetailed deer becomes a "visual miracle" in which a mystic participation ties the whitetail of the wilderness with the hunter, a human/animal tie grounded in spiritual unity.

When man and the whitetail die, Faulkner believed, they are free to do what they love most: to participate in a deer hunt in the sky, or as Faulkner says, in "the long challenge and the long chase."

In Faulkner's deer hunting stories, the hunter joins the whitetail in sacred space which is, was, and will be. The deer forest becomes a place where endings are also beginnings, where mortality dissolves into a recurrent cycle of death and rebirth.

For William Faulkner, the ritual of deer hunting reaches its highest level when it becomes an initiation rite, or rite of passage, a holy occupation ultimately played out in sacred space.

A.F. Wileden Collection.

MEMORIES FROM BUCKSHOT INC.

"A much-debated question at the present time revolves around the probable future of the group. Can it survive the aging cycle? Is the organization structure sufficiently flexible to make continuity possible?"

— *A.F. Wileden,*
The Buckshot Story, *1928-1972*

Deer hunters in camps and clubs have asked Arthur F. Wileden's questions for time immemorial. Few deer camps or deer clubs survive the aging process, especially when we talk in terms of 50 years or more. Buckshot Inc. represents one of those rare, quality deer camps that not only displayed exemplary hunter behavior in the field, but was still in existence more than 70 years after its formation. As a result, the Buckshot tradition still continued when this book was written in 2001, operating as the A.C. Wollin Sr. Game Lodge Inc., with hosts Roger and Carole Wollin.

Courtesy of Roger Wollin.

Jess Sharp with her .30-30 Winchester Model '94 and a quality buck, 1930.

One realizes how rarely deer camps enjoy such longevity when examining deer-camp questions in a study made by rural sociologist Tom Heberlein in 1981. Heberlein's survey in Wisconsin looked at many aspects of hunter behavior, but when hunters were asked if they hunted from a deer camp, only 52 percent said yes. Further, only 42 percent of those saying yes said they hunted from a shack. When asked if the founding members still came to the camp, 89 percent said no. When asked when their group started hunting, 40 percent indicated 1940 or earlier.

The Buckshot Inc. story had its informal beginnings in 1928, when two avid deer hunters — Manley Sharp, a Douglas County, Wis., agricultural agent, and Albert C. Wollin Sr., founder of the Wollin Silo and Equipment Co. of Lake Mills — began buying land near Cable, Wis., for deer hunting. They eventually bought 480 acres in sections 6 and 8 in the township of Cable near Dawn Lake in Bayfield County. The camp incorporated under Wisconsin statutes in March 1956 for the stated purpose of "hunting, fishing and other recreational activities."

Landmark sites on the property carry special names and meanings, and they're duly recorded in the *Buckshot Record Book*: Conlin's Ridge Trail, Kruse's Woods, Lerche's Lakes, Cable Hills, Buckshot Swamp, Sugar Bush Road, Boar's Nest, Ole Lake, Big Brook Swamp, Trout Lake, Tobacco Ridge, Rogan's Trail, Dawn Lake and Rogan's Shack. The latest generation of Buckshot deer

Courtesy of Roger Wollin.

Above, Gif "Butch," Al Wollin Sr. and Paul Dehnert prepare to return to civilization with four bucks and several Christmas trees, 1946. Right, Professor "Ham" Bruhn and Al Wollin Sr. pose with two 8-pointers shot by Bruhn and Professor B.C. Jorns, 1946.

Courtesy of Roger Wollin.

hunters adds new names of their own, such as Susan's Pines and Barb's Bush. Women have hunted the Buckshot as early as 1930, as we see in some black and white photos of Jess Sharp with her .30-30 Model '94 Winchester.

Buckshot Inc. was special in at least two important respects, as we learn from the memoirs of a founding member, Arthur F. Wileden. In "The Buckshot Story, 1928-1972," Wileden — a former professor in the department of rural sociology at the University of Wisconsin in Madison — wrote:

"It was a strait-laced group with great emphasis on hunter safety. Liquor and gambling were not permitted. Also, one of the wives did most of the cooking and someone almost always said grace at the always big evening meal. I recall one of my fellow faculty members saying he didn't think there

was a deer hunting camp like that in North America."

As the years passed, the number of hunters steadily increased until the hunt became the year's major event. In late November 1972 — when the gunsmoke cleared at the end of the 41st deer season at Buckshot Inc. — 230 white-tailed bucks had gone to the meatpole, or "deer tree," an average of 5.6 per year. The camp's historical record was kept by Gerald Annin (1903-1991), a professor in poul-

try husbandry at UW-Madison for 38 years. Further, in a letter to the author, Buckshot member Gordon Gottschalk (1922-2000), reported that between 1972 and 1986, Buckshot's hunters downed another 102 deer, bringing the camp's total to 415, including antlerless deer.

In his memoirs on the Buckshot story, Wileden analyzed the group's shooting performance:

"One of the most striking things is the preponderance of 8-point bucks taken, about 40 percent of the total buck kill (not counting spikes). Judging from weights, it is apparent that 8-point bucks are usually in their prime. If we include the kill of bucks with more than eight points, over two-thirds of the bucks killed by this group of hunters would be included. These were mostly mature bucks.

"It appears the party permit idea, first established in Wisconsin in 1957 and later again in 1964, seemed to have only a gradual effect on the group's buck-hunting success. But the record certainly argues for a rather carefully group-controlled or state-controlled party-permit system.

"The heaviest bucks killed by this group of hunters were a 195-pound 10-pointer in 1948, a 190-pound 12-pointer and a 187-pound 8-pointer in 1940. The closest approach to these in later seasons was a 185-pound 14-pointer in 1955, and a 184-pound 10-pointer in 1963. These are field-dressed weights, and the deer were all promptly weighed on a reliable scale when brought into camp. As we look at the weights of all of the bucks

killed, it appears they are slightly lighter in weight in more recent seasons. Maybe the shortage of available food supply in the area is taking its toll, as lumbering has about stopped and the trees are getting bigger. The percent of hunter success for bucks also seems to be declining."

Buckshot Inc. kept an accurate record of all deer-camp activities. From the group's deer-camp record book — a 12-by-14-inch buckskin-clad volume — we learn the first group consisted of eight hunters in 1928. That was the year the Wisconsin Department of Conservation required deer hunters to wear official conservation buttons while deer hunting. (The button was required until 1932.) The eight hunters shot six bucks that year for a 75 percent success rate — a remarkable feat given the region's low buck densities at the time.

A.C. Wollin Sr. (1890-1976), a die-hard buck hunter and camp leader, shot his buck Dec. 2, 1928, with his old, cherished Winchester .32 Special. Wollin connected on a running shot 165 yards north of Jim's Tree. This enthusiastic buck hunter and founding father of Buckshot Inc. set a tremendous mark for this region: In 13 consecutive deer seasons, he tagged 12 white-tailed bucks with his trusty .32 Special.

As the Buckshot hunters continued to bring home venison, A.C. Wollin Sr. reported the results of each deer hunt to *The Lake Mills Leader* news-

Through the Pines. **Ned Smith. Oil on canvas, 1979.**

paper. On Dec. 2, 1943, the paper announced, "Hunters Return From North With Much Venison." The paper reported 25 deer hunters at Buckshot Inc. and the Sharp & Wollin Game Lodge shot 25 deer, including seven bucks during the 1942 deer season. This was the year the Conservation Commission first required back tags, a tradition that remains strong in Wisconsin's deer woods. Another article in *The Lake Mills Leader* published in December 1947 noted that with 15 inches of snow and temperatures of minus 20 degrees, 25 hunters bagged seven bucks, one bear and one wolf.

On Thursday, Dec. 2, 1948, *The Lake Mills Leader* observed that with hunting conditions extremely unfavorable, the Buckshot encampment netted a 47 percent average in getting deer during the 1948 either-sex season. In a headline story, "All Hunters At Cable Lodge Got Deer," published Dec. 1, 1949, *The Lake Mills Leader* reported 31 Buckshot hunters bagged 31 deer for a 100 percent success rate.

The *Buckshot Record Book,* which is made out of cedar and buckskin, lists the names of all hunters present, their deer sightings, unusual stories and circumstances, when and where hunters shot their deer, time of day, weather conditions, method of hunting, temperatures, wind direction, dressed weights, antler measurements, and deer camp menus. The book also reveals that in the 41 years between 1928 and 1972, more than 144 people had attended camp at least once.

The Buckshot group consisted of 12 founding members (individual shareholders), and 19 families, which became a closely knit group. The 12 original members were professor Gerald E. Annin, Albert C. Wollin Sr., Sid Wolff, professor G. William Longenecker, professor Arthur F. Wileden, A.C. (Bud) Wollin Jr., professor O.B. Combs, professor Bruce L. Cartter, professor B.C. Jorns, Verne V. Varney, Raymond "Bloomie" Helmer Sr., and professor Hjalmar D. "Ham" Bruhn, who hunted the Buckshot for more than 50 years.

This record book itself, designed with the craftsmanship of member Verne Varney (1892-1976), a leader of Wisconsin's 4-H program, remains a cherished artifact of the Buckshot group. In 2001, it continued to help break in neophytes at the A.C. Wollin Game Lodge Inc. As each tenderfoot joined the camp, he generally read the log and learned the camp's history.

A magnificent colored drawing of a 9-point whitetail graces the cover. The drawing is an origi-

Rob Wegner Photo Collection.

A.F. Wileden Collection.

Top left, the original Buckshot record book made of cedar and buckskin with a 9-pointer drawn by Buckshot member Byron Jorns. Left, Jorns often painted while hunting deer.

A.F. Wileden Collection.

nal by professor Bryon Jorns (1899-1958), a well-known University of Wisconsin artist who often entered the woods with his easel instead of his rifle. Many of Jorns' beautiful North Woods deer hunting paintings turned up in the homes of Buckshot Inc. members.

The Buckshot Record Book contains an official "Deer Hunters' Certificate," which was issued to all 12 members for their ability to come home from deer hunts without a buck. The certificate also granted them the right to shoot off their mouths about the big "horns" on bucks they missed. The certificate was signed by President Spike Horn and Secretary Buck Fever.

Birthdays and weddings within the Buckshot group were celebrated and remembered. The featured social event of the year, however, was the deer hunters' dinner the Saturday night before opening day. All hunters, past and present, and their families were invited.

Sid Wolf studies topographical maps as professors "Ham" Bruhn and Gerry Annin talk deer in front of the Buckshot gun rack, 1954.

Besides venison, this menu frequently included bear, moose, antelope and elk.

"Hundreds of pictures were shown, stories told and even secrets shared," Wileden reported in *A Lifetime of Hunting and Fishing Experiences* (1982). "The eating together, the sharing of experiences and just being together was always looked forward to with great expectancy. Without it, the Buckshot story would not have been complete."

While many Buckshot hunters went to their "happy hunting grounds" during the camp's first 40 years, it's remarkable this group survived the generation gap, with sons, sons-in-law and grandsons perpetuating the Buckshot tradition into the 21st century.

Professor Robert Jackson — a psychologist at the University of Wisconsin-LaCrosse, studied deer-hunter behavior during the 1980s. He suggested that if a deer camp creates a meaningful social experience for everyone, hunters will be able to count its longevity in terms of decades. In his research, Jackson concluded: "The classical deer camp has tremendous power over its members. Its cohesiveness and productivity build group bonds that demand conformity to group standards."

Buckshot Inc. fit that description. Seven professors from UW-Madison belonged as founding members, and the camp's standards of behavior remained high, thus contributing to more than a half-century of deer hunting camaraderie. Many of these experiences took place near the old Buckshot cabin in Section 6. This cabin is an impressive, traditional structure built of tamarack logs cut in the area. The walls' logs measured 18 inches thick at the butt end and were 28 to 32 feet in length.

As a rural sociologist, Wileden concluded it's impossible to operate a classic deer camp without a cook who possesses gourmet, "venisoniferous" tastes and talents.

Wileden wrote: "I am sure a major reason why we so fittingly called our deer camp a Health Resort was because of the well-planned and substantial meals — especially the evening meals, every one of which would pass for a Thanksgiving Dinner. The hunters, usually Sid Wolff and Gerry Annin, take care of breakfast. And the noon meal is sandwiches in the woods, often more ham or roast beef and cheese than bread, toasted over a warming noon-day fire. But the evening meal is really a feast, and this is where the cooks take over. For nineteen years, Josephine Annin was the house mother. She not only prepared the evening dinner but pampered the hunters when mentally bruised or developed a cold or a headache, and repaired their frequently ripped and torn trousers. In latter years Mac Wolff took over, starting under Jo's able tutelage. Once we have our cook, a large part of the success of the camp for that year is assured."

When lunch time came in the late-autumn deer woods, it was time for Art — whether alone on still-hunts, with a buddy or between large drives — to build his legendary small fire, toast his sandwich and chew on a turkey wing.

The group's communal life was often rustic. Mel Ellis, a famous outdoor writer for the *Milwaukee Journal*, characterized the cabin after a visit in the early 1960s.

"Even before I crossed the threshold I felt at peace with myself and the world. I literally could heave a great sigh as though a burden of physical proportions had been lifted from my back. That was the kind of camp it was, a place that shuts out the world and all the worry that goes with it. It

A.F. Wileden Collection.

stood in good deer country, but I am sure it would have been the same under the sun of the Sahara or within reach of a high tide.

"This deer camp was a wind howling down the chimney, snow swirling past the windows, trees groaning in the wind and snow squeaking underneath along the path to the little two-holer. ...

"This camp was 5-pound chunks of American Swiss and Cheddar cheese standing on the cutting board, beans browned with sugar and covered with

Members and guests of Buckshot Inc. always posed for a final photo in front of the "deer tree" before packing their gear and heading home.

salt pork waiting on the stove. It was rifles standing in a corner, red clothing steaming on chair backs, tiny streams of water running across the floor from boots by the door, gloves drying in an open oven. There was frost creeping up the windowpane, snow piling high around the woodpile, tracks up the trail sifting full and fading."

As with most deer camps, the Buckshot group loved to tell stories, as did Ellis. And, like most camps, their stories tended to acquire inches of fiction with each recitation, bordering at times on malarkey. Consider the story of big Al, who fired one quick shot across a long canyon at a rapidly departing "Harvey Wall Hanger." When one of the younger hunters ran up to him and shouted, "Did you get him?" Al calmly replied, "You heard me shoot, boy, didn't you?"

Or consider the old nonmember they met on a cold November day, who had a gun in one hand and a cane in the other. When a Buckshot member asked what a deer hunter was doing in the woods with a white cane, the old man replied, "When I can't see 'em, I'll feel for 'em."

Or how about the story of professor O.B. Combs, a great bear hunter from the North Country, who apparently had to negotiate with the Bear Haulers' Union to get his bear out of Big Brook Swamp. Professor Combs, who worked in the department of horticulture at UW-Madison, was reportedly so impressed with his accomplishment on Nov. 25, 1947, that he mailed a postcard home to his wife with this inscription:

Courtesy of Roger Wollin.

"God made the mountains and he made the valleys, He made the giant oak and the little blades of grass, He made the oceans and the little drops of water, He made me and he made a Bear Hunter."

Many legendary deer camps had a literary tradition of high-class spoofery, and Buckshot Inc. was no exception. On Nov. 9, 1958, Major I.M.A. Stinker, "Executive Secretary of the High committee on Skullduggery," issued the following citation, or "Ode to Combs":

"*BE IT KNOWN now and preserved for all time for all to see that EVERY DOG SHALL HAVE HIS DAY.*

"*AFTER many years of PATIENT AND PERSEVERING SUFFERING OF THE JIBES, SNIDE REMARKS, and GENUINE INSULTS and even QUESTIONS regarding his political INTELLIGENCE and INTEGRITY by sympathizers of the SELF-PROCLAIMED, non-communist ORDER of a seeming MINORITY GROUP as of November 4, 1958, our TRUE BLUE, LOYAL, and STEADFAST DEMOCRAT has come into HIS OWN.*

"*As a SYMBOL of the HIGH ESTEEM in which we now hold this LOYAL DEMOCRAT OF BUCKSHOT INCORPORATED and all its SUBSIDIARIES including THE MAIN LODGE, THE LOWER CABIN, CONLIN'S RIDGE, THE NARROWS, CABLE HILLS, THE NORTHWEST TRAIL, TOBACCO RIDGE, KRUSE'S CROSS HAULS, LAKE MILL, SHOREWOOD HILLS, AND ITS SUBURB, Madison, Wisconsin, we wish to present to O.B. (the bear hole looker) COMBS this solid GOLD-PLATED EMBLEM of our GOOD FAITH. Let him always wear it that he may continue to STAND OUT among us.*

"*Approved for release and publication by the HIGH COMMITTEE on SKULLDUGGERY.*"

And, of course, we must not forget the story of what happened on the northwest trail when O.B. wounded a giant buck that member Gordy Gottschalk tracked to its death. Wileden documented the story:

"Gordy picked up the track and followed it all the way past the lodge, down the camp road where he (and the buck) met Al driving into camp, up into the Cable Hills, and then back

Some of the North Woods scenery around the camp.

A.F. Wileden Collection.

The old Buckshot Inc. cabin in Wisconsin's Bayfield County is a traditional structure built from tamarack logs 18 inches thick at the butt and 28 to 32 feet long. Circa 1952.

again to within a couple hundred yards of camp. There, with his last remaining rounds of ammunition, he finally killed it. It is reported that Gordy and his buck were both so exhausted with their all-day, nine-mile game of peek-a-boo, that they had agreed to finish it off as close as possible to the cabin."

Not only did Buckshot members like to tell deer hunting stories, they liked to read them. Many of them read and reread Gordon MacQuarrie's deer hunting story "You've Got to Suffer," and quoted its memorable lines:

"The snowshoes creaked. I followed the thoroughfare edge. There was ice out from shore forty yards at my right. At my left and ahead of me was thick cover. ...

"Then I saw a fresh track. You know how it is — that virgin white scar of a hoof in snow, so unlike the settled, stiffened track of twelve hours before. ...

"That track was big and brand-new. It was a mark left by a critter moving exactly the way I wanted it to move — straight north toward the Old Man. ...

"It went dead on toward a rendezvous with a Winchester .30-30 carbine held by a very steady old gentleman. ...

"Finally I saw him. He was across an opening, perhaps a hundred yards off. He was big and dim. No question now what he was. He was 'he.' His rack went up and back like branches on an old oak. I might have had one quick fling at him, but why chance it? The Old Man was waiting, and it was better to move that deer into the open Norway grove. Then, if the first one didn't clip him, there would be other chances.

"I went along. I knew that terrain as well as the buck knew it — almost as well as the Old Man knows it. Pretty soon, up ahead, there would be a shot. Just one shot, it ought to be. That would be the Old Man's 150 grains of lead and copper going to its destination. Then silence — the sort of quiet after one shot that means so much to a deer hunter."

Wileden said Buckshot members also read the great deer and deer hunting literature of the day: Aldo Leopold's scientific studies on deer population dynamics and management, Ernie Swift's *A History of Wisconsin Deer* (1946), Larry Koller's *Shots at Whitetails* (1948), Walter P. Taylor's well-documented *The Deer of North America* (1956), Otis Bersing's encyclopedic *A Century of Wisconsin Deer* (1966), and Burton Dahlberg and Ralph Guettinger's academic monograph *The White-Tailed Deer in Wisconsin* (1956).

B y the mid-1980s, Buckshot Inc. reached a critical stage in its history because of inflation, rapidly rising land values, and aging and deaths among its membership. In a letter Nov. 24, 1978, Wileden posed the crucial question that haunted the group: "Are we still thinking of ourselves as a deer hunting group or as a business

organization with recreational land to sell?" As more members went down their final trail, Buckshot Inc. died May 1, 1986, when the remaining members liquidated the corporation and sold Buckshot's 480 acres to Sam Johnson of the Johnson Wax Co. of Racine, Wis.

In the last chapter of *A Lifetime of Hunting and Fishing Experiences*, titled "WHY? WHY? WHY?" Wileden asked the members why they hunted deer. The most frequent response involved the desire to get and keep as close to nature as possible. Al Wollin talked about returning to the "natural universe." Bloomie Helmer, a retired chemist from

The A.C. Wollin Sr. Game Lodge as it looks today. The lodge continues in the Buckshot tradition under the leadership of Roger Wollin.

Photos courtesy of Roger Wollin.

Wauwatosa, desired to become part of "God's natural world" instead of civilization.

Escape from modern-life pressures constituted the second most common reason for deer hunting. "We go hunting in an attempt to escape the tension of the world of the organizational man," wrote professor "Bill" Longenecker, director of UW-Madison's arboretum from 1933 to 1967, and the founder and chairman of the university's department of landscape architecture.

The third most popular reason included an intimate search for new experiences. "Looking for something different," is how one member explained it. That was followed by the need for physical exercise, which Wileden expressed this way: "I have always felt that the hunting season, particularly the deer hunting season, was the fitting climax to a moderately physically active spring and summer and the proper conditioner for a less physically active winter. Often have I said that it was the fall build-up that tided me over a winter period of relative physical dormancy until spring again arouses our dormant natural surroundings and awakens us to a new life of growing things about us."

Yet, even after a lifetime of hunting deer at Buckshot Inc., Wileden never believed he adequately answered his own question, why? why? why? But he acknowledged that a certain intangible element exists in deer hunting that escapes verbal or literary expression:

"It seems to be related to the universe itself like storms and fair weather or the rising and setting of the sun. Underneath it all is not only a desire to be a part of something, but also a desire to preserve something."

While researching the camp's background for his *History of Buckshot, Incorporated, 1956-1986,* Gordy Gottschalk, a Lake Mills farmer, found the following poem among the camp's records. Written by the Rev. W.H. Thompson of Blue River, Wis., in November 1944, the poem expresses the feelings of most of the camp's hunters:

Below left, one of the 1999 deer hunters at the A.C. Wollin Sr. Game Lodge. Below right, Roger Wollin, lifelong member of Buckshot Inc., and hunt master of A.C. Wollin Sr. Game Lodge.

Buck Fever

Goldie Foot is a wise old buck
Who is either charmed or has great luck.
One day a hunter, with mighty stride,
Set out to get old Goldie's hide.
Out across valley, swamp and hill
This hunter marched as if on drill.
The day was still, the light was good,
When came Goldie from out the wood.
The hunter stood as if in a trance,
For here was his much desired chance.
He raised his trusty Savage high,
And scanned the sights with gleaming eye.
Like the eye that bumped the open door,
And must find an excuse for being sore
This hunter's rifle didn't shoot true?
So he missed, as many hunters do.
I have hunted this fleet-footed game,
Until I was weary, hungry and lame.
If when evening comes I have had a shot,
The day has been good whether I missed or not.
To tread the forest and find my way,
Where I never passed until that day.
Is a triumph that always brings a thrill,
Greater than to have made a kill.
So when next season opens on buck,
I'll be burning up to try my luck.
The wily buck may avoid my gun,
But he can't keep me from having fun.

Photos courtesy of Roger Wollin.

Courtesy of Roger Wollin.

The 1999 deer hunters at the A.C. Wollin Sr. Game Lodge Inc.

Every deer camp has its mythic buck like Goldie Foot. Roger Wollin, founder of Fiberdome Inc., follows in his father's footsteps in pursuit of old Goldie Foot, and he took Buckshot Inc.'s spirit and deer hunting traditions into the 21st century with class and dignity. He still places standers at many of the same cherished spots his father did before him, and conducts the same time-honored deer drives in the eternal deer hunt. The camp's record book continues with stories, detailed information and deer hunting photos. Every evening meal still rises to the heights of a Thanksgiving feast, with camp cook Glenda Jalowitz displaying her cooking talents. After offering a prayer, deer hunters from Illinois, New Jersey, Indiana, Virginia and Wisconsin partake in deer camp camaraderie at its finest. Now and then a Boone and Crockett buck even graces the "deer tree."

When looking at the history of Buckshot Inc., and its ensuing traditions at the A.C. Wollin Sr. Game Lodge Inc., we're reminded of the timelessness of deer hunting. As my friend John Howard, a die-hard buck hunter, once said:

"Nothing changes.
Only the actors in the drama.
The plot remains the same.
The deer roams the hills. The man follows it.
Only the name of the man changes.
The deer changes too. But only the individual,
not the species."

Although the names of this deer camp changed over time, as did the names of the hunters, the spirit and tradition of Buckshot Inc. lives on in the minds of those who still deer hunt Cable Hills, Conlin's Ridge Trail, Kruse's Woods, Buckshot Swamp and all those other sacred places. This is especially true of Roger Wollin. He still dreams of the original Buckshot group and their great deer hunting stories, which were told in the light of kerosene lanterns. As he dreams, he soaks up the sights, odors, tastes and sounds of Buckshot's popping bowls of snowy white popcorn.

TEN POINT CLUB

"In the American South, deer hunting in particular verges on an organized religion. ... It is a hobby that often borders on an obsession, and is particularly entrenched in the Mississippi Delta."

— Alan Huffman,
Ten Point: Deer Camp in the Mississippi Delta, 1977.

Florence Huffman. Courtesy Mississippi Department of Archives and History.

Baying hounds, deer hunting horns and their semi-religious overtones signaled a pleasurable and grand diversion for hunters in the Mississippi Delta as early as the 1830s. Planters, journalists, naturalists and sportsmen documented the deep-swamp excitement of the deer chase and deer-camp life in sporting journals of the time, such as *The American Field, Forest and Stream, Spirit of the Times* and the *American Turf Register.*

In an article titled "Deer Hunting in the Yazoo Swamp," a Mississippi deer hunter penned an ode to those who wandered the Delta's swamps and hills in endless pursuit of deer. The article was published April 6, 1844, in William T. Porter's *Spirit of the Times,* and was written by "Yazoo," a "thorough-going swamper." He wrote:

"I have often, when a boy ... stalked them and dropped them in their tracks. I have of a dark night, with frying-pan upon my shoulder filled with blazing pine knots, sought their haunts, and when their gleaming eye-balls caught my gaze have killed them by dozens. ... with my rifle have piled them up in cords! ... taken them with my double barrel right and left — on one occasion two at a crack, making them throw somersaults in the most fantastic style."

But Yazoo admitted he never dreamed of flushing them with pointers and popping them from horseback as they arose from the thickets.

But that's what he found himself doing on a Mississippi deer hunt the morning of Feb. 25, 1844, in the Yazoo Swamp.

"Our party consisted of ten, mounted upon the soberest hacks the plantation could muster, selected with the view of shooting from their backs without the risk of a fall. ... Bang! — bang! — went two barrels in quick succession on our left. 'My liquor,' cried the huntsman who had fired; — it was our guide, with a head like Bacchus and a frame like Hercules. 'I have drawn the first blood,' continued he, 'and am entitled to the treat.' All awarded it to him as we rode up and saw the beautiful doe stretch her fleet limbs, to rise no more."

Yazoo wrote that in five days of hunting deer in the Yazoo Swamp, the party of 10 huntsmen killed 31 deer besides other game.

In an earlier article titled "Deer Hunting in Mississippi," published Nov. 19, 1842, in the *Spirit of the Times,* a Mississippi deer hunter named "Boone" described a lively deer-camp hunt on the Pearl River five miles east of Brandon.

"We struck a light and rolled our bone for Coffee Bogue — pitched our tent, and among the deer we commenced the work of death in earnest! ...

"Sometimes we surrounded a thicket, each man at his post, anxiously waiting until the deer should emerge from the ruff. Perhaps

Louie Brame with a 12-pointer.

Florence Huffman. Courtesy of Mississippi Department of Archives and History.

right opposite where you stood you would hear a gun go 'bang.' In an instant 'bang,' 'bang,' and then a yell — ride round, and behold there lay the deer, ready to be borne to the camp. This was not always the case, for sometimes I let off old carbine, and the deer showed me his white tail and struck a lick to the tune of 'Over the hills and far away.' "

Boone detailed the deer camp's evening bill of fare: "venison steak, roasted melts, kidneys fried, turkey fricasseed, turkey's breast fried, warm corn bread and strong coffee. Now, if this does not set your mouths all a-foggin, hang such taste as you have, I say."

In seven days of deer hunting, Boone reported six deer hunters skinned 44 deer.

In another colorful story in the *Spirit of the Times* of March 13, 1856, a cotton-plantation owner on the Yazoo River, "G.W.P.," wrote that the Yazoo Swamp was filled with deer and with "deer hunters as noble as men ever get to be." He hunted deer with "as fine a pack of loud-mouthed dogs as ever ran an antlered buck, or clenched the haunches of a splendid deer." Judge and Jury — two noble dogs — led his pack on many a gallant run and chase.

During this time, deer hunting remained an essential part of life in Mississippi. Mainstream magazines covered the topic for their general audiences. People worldwide considered the Delta to harbor America's most enthusiastic deer hunters. Connoisseurs of the chase, such as "Frank Forester" — the foremost authority on hunting in the mid-19th century — glorified Mississippi as a deer hunting mecca in *Field Sports of the United States* (1860):

"In order ... to enjoy deer hunting in anything like perfection ... we must go into ... Mississippi. There we find the gentlemen of the land, not pent up in cities, but dwelling on their estates; there we find hunters, *par amours*, if I may so express myself, and packs of hounds maintained regularly, and hunted with all legitimate accompaniments of well-blown bugle and well-whooped halloo; with mounted cavaliers, fearlessly riding

through brush, through briar, over flood, over mire ... as desperately, for the first blood, or the kill, as they do in old England, in Leicester or Northampton, to the Quron hounds, or the Squire's lady pack. This is the Sport, par excellence."

Deer hunting in the South during the 19th century maintained a dignity not found in other parts of the country. It entailed a long-lasting legacy of land, family and tradition; and of honor, pride and independence. It required intimate knowledge of a specific terrain, and a fidelity to a "core area" of whitetail country inherited from past generations and a lifetime in the deer woods. Neighboring deer hunting clubs often vied with each other; the losers paying for a dinner with fine wine, brandy, whiskey and barbecued venison.

Nowhere is that deer hunting culture more ingrained than Mississippi, where the deer camp is intertwined with the state's literature and culture. The word "deer" dominates the names of places and topography throughout the Delta: Deer Slough, Deer Creek, Deer Creek Road, Deer Island, Deer Lake and Deer Ridge. In the article "The Horn of the Hunter: On the Banks of the Yazoo," (*Forest and Stream*, Jan. 6, 1900) a Wall Street banker who identified himself as "C.H.," claimed he could scent white-tailed deer in the postmark "Yazoo, Miss."

In his description of "The Four Oaks" deer camp on the Yazoo River, C.H. wrote that his deer-hunting buddies from Mississippi often abandoned reality when telling deer hunting stories around the campfire. Tales of earlier deer hunts merged quickly into the realm of mythology. In his sketch of shooting a buck, C.H. was not undone by the hyperbole of his Mississippi comrades:

"A few moments after reaching my position, I heard Preacher open and my nerves commenced to tingle in anticipation, and presently a crash in the cane to my left quickened my attention. All that I could see of the game was his flag, and rather than spoil a possible fair shot for the

Florence Huffman. Courtesy of Mississippi Department of Archives and History.

Major, I waited. After passing me he stopped, and in a moment, much to my surprise and joy, I saw him coming toward me and to the north. The specter to me was splendid — the largest buck I had ever seen in the woods, with nose up and antlers well down on his shoulders, parting the cane and thicket. I fired, and he fell as if stricken to death. ...

"Preacher suddenly appeared and tackled his fallen quarry, who with one last effort sprang to his feet and dashed toward the Major, missing him and striking a tree with such force as to break off a considerable part of his fine antlers. By this time the whole pack appeared, and in his frantic efforts to get away he dashed about, striking trees and making the situation threatening to the Major and me. The excitement was intense, and as he made a blind charge at me I fired again, striking him in the eye and silencing him forever."

After field dressing the buck, C.H. filled his pipe and sat on a fallen tree to contemplate the scene. He drew from his hunter's coat a volume by Balzac, *The Deputy From Arcis*, and passed an

Al Carr and an unidentified man with deer and P.K. Huffman's horse, Annie.

hour or so with good company, listening to the howling deer hounds and the horns of the hunters on the banks of the Yazoo.

In his two-volume work, *The South-West. By A Yankee* (1835), historian Joseph Holt Ingraham (1809-1860) provides one of the earliest accounts of coursing deer in Mississippi. This was a spirit-stirring scene at the Woodbourne Plantation near Natchez, with hunters using horses, hounds and horns. Woodbourne, a distinguished New Jersey lawyer turned Southern planter, had shot 27 bucks, with rows of notches cut into his hunting horn testifying to the tally. Woodbourne personified the virtues of thoroughbred deer hunters: patience, unwearied spirits, uncommon nerve and great presence of mind.

After placing his Yankee visitor on his stand, Ingraham heard "the distant baying of dogs, in that peculiar note with which they open when they have roused their game. The chorus of canine voices soon grew louder and more violent.

Florence Huffman. Courtesy Mississippi Department of Archives and History.

Although whitetails were scarce in the Delta during the 1940s, Mississippi deer hunters downed impressive bucks at Ten Point.

As they awoke the echoes of the forest and came down upon us like a storm, my heart leaped and the blood coursed merrily in my veins. ... All at once, with a crash and a bound, a noble stag, with his head laid back upon his shoulders, crossed our line at the remotest stand, and disappeared into the thick woods along the river. The dogs followed like meteors."

The Mississippi Delta's colorful deer-hunting history can be traced back to those early sporting journals, and culminate, of course, in the deer-hunting narratives of William Faulkner. Especially colorful is Faulkner's deer-hunting story "Delta Autumn" in *Go Down, Moses* (1940). After reading this story, no one can forget how Old Sam Fathers initiated the 12-year-old boy into manhood and the deer hunting

fraternity as they stood by a giant cypress tree in the deep swamp:

"There was something running in Sam Fathers' veins which ran in the veins of the buck and they stood there against the tremendous trunk, the old man and the boy of twelve, and there was nothing but the dawn and then suddenly the buck was there, smoke-colored out of nothing, magnificent with speed, and Sam Fathers said, 'Now. Shoot quick and shoot slow,' and the gun leveled without hurry and crashed and he walked to the buck lying still intact and still in the shape of the magnificent speed and he bled it with his own knife and Sam Fathers dipped his hands in the hot blood and marked his face forever while he stood trying not to tremble, humbly and with pride too though the boy of twelve had been unable to phrase it then, 'I slew you; my bearing must not shame your quitting life. My conduct forever onward must become your death."

In his commitment to the deer's spirit, Faulkner comes close to apologizing to the deer and dedicates himself to hunt ethically and thoughtfully thereafter. Like Aldo Leopold and Theodore Roosevelt, Faulkner described deer hunting as a quasi-religious activity of mythic and spiritual meaning directly connected to the wilderness. His deer camp was located near Onward on Steele Bayou, not far above Vicksburg on the Big Sunflower River. Roosevelt also hunted deer on Steele Bayou in 1902.

Within this geographic and cultural context, one of the most legendary deer camps of all time emerged: the Ten Point Deer Club.

Located in one of the South's great wilderness areas — the Steele Bayou wilderness of Mississippi's Issaquena County — the Ten Point Deer Club became a remote gathering place from 1927 to 1962 for lawyers, doctors, businessmen, their employees and their wives; as well as cooks, mechanics, fishermen, housewives, handymen and a handful of backwoods men. This diverse group had one thing in common: They loved to hunt deer and gather food from the Delta's dense, wet and inhospitable canebrakes and cypress forests. They would probably never have come together under other circumstances.

Everyone participated in the camp's communal work assignments. This deer club, as with many deer camps, served as a common denominator, overriding all social-class distinctions. The social bonds that characterized their off-season dinners at hotels in Jackson, Miss., were even more pronounced in the deer woods.

Over the years, more than a hundred people participated in the Ten Point deer hunts. Many of these hunters viewed camp as a place to lose yourself and be alone with others. Other hunters saw camp as a place to come to terms with your own insignificance. Some members loved its traditions and the excitement of the unexpected. Others used it as an excuse to disappear into the woods with friends. The deer hunt and camp life for the Ten Point Deer Club became a way of life, a habit of mind, a cultural institution and a respectable outlet for excitement and self-indulgence. In their re-enactment of their cultural history, many camp members returned to the Pleistocene.

Deer hunter Hatfield returning from the Ten Point Deer Club with his deer aboard the Yazoo River Ferry, 1939.

Florence Huffman. Courtesy Mississippi Department of Archives and History.

Under the leadership of Paul King Huffman and his wife, Florence — known as Mama Florence — the Ten Point Deer Club became the most thoroughly documented camp in the history of American deer hunting. Florence knew the deer hunting heritage is a state of mind, and that it can survive only if it is nurtured with photos, films and journals. Florence was a deer hunter and amateur photographer, and she took more than 4,000 black-and-white photographs on all aspects of camp life — 1,500 of which now repose in the Mississippi Department of Archives and History. In addition, the Center for the Study of Southern Culture in Oxford, Miss., has 20 color films in 16 mm showing Ten Point's deer hunts.

In 1997, Florence's grandson, Alan Huffman, published a history of the camp: *Ten Point: Deer Camp in the Mississippi Delta.* From his detailed portrait, we learn that 10 to 15 deer hunters took their stands with shotguns and buckshot as Redbone and Walker hounds chased the deer. During the early 1930s, the club hunted only bucks.

The excitement of deer hunts with horses, hounds and buckshot played itself out across the South during the first three decades of the 1900s. In his *Looking Back At The Boykin Hunting Club* (1984), Henry D. Boykin II describes the uproar in its universal dimensions:

"A sudden uproar came from the hounds. Bootie saw the deer and gave his unsurpassed jump-whoop, followed by, 'Look out fer 'im!' The hounds were suddenly at full cry. The combined noise of hounds, horses and drivers created frenzied excitement, and the effect was electric. I expected a big buck to explode from the undergrowth any moment, and I strained eyes and ears for the chance — that became a shot, and a second shot, by the next stander. Disappointment! The wild symphony ended, the dogs stopped, so the deer was dead, and the drivers' horns rang out

The Ten Point Clubhouse in the late 1940s after a rare snowfall in the Mississippi Delta.

Florence Huffman. Courtesy of Mississippi Department of Archives and History.

A group shot at Jack McIntyre's Ice Plant. This photo ran in the *Jackson Daily News*, commemorating the 1948 season.

Florence Huffman. Courtesy of Mississippi Department of Archives and History.

to bring the dogs together for another start. It was a well-rehearsed performance by those veterans, a pleasure to hear, and I was consoled by knowing that the next drive would offer another chance."

In the early 1900s, hunting whitetails in the Delta was difficult for members of any club. According to Mississippi deer biologist Robert Nobel, game surveys from that era indicate deer lived in 34 of Mississippi's 82 counties, with a total herd numbering less than 1,000. In 1929, Aldo Leopold reported that only small herds remained in limited parts of the Delta, and in the Pearl and Pascagoula River Swamps. According to Billy Carter, a Jackson, Miss., attorney and club member, a hunter could hunt 20 years without getting a deer.

Yet, despite low deer densities, the Ten Point Deer Club managed to bag some large bucks, and the deer population would soon improve. In 1932, the Mississippi Legislature established the

Mississippi Game and Fish Commission. By 1940, an aggressive deer restoration project funded by the Pittman-Robertson Act was well underway. During the next 40 years, researchers trapped thousands of deer in North Carolina, Texas, Mexico and Wisconsin and restocked them in Mississippi.

Fortunately for the deer, wildfires followed the "cut-out-and-get-out" policy of Delta logging operations from 1900 to 1925. The wildfires burned thousands of acres, removed the residual timber stands, and opened up the forest floor. This created favorable conditions for second-growth timber and provided ideal deer habitat. The herd quickly rebounded to the satisfaction of the club's growing membership.

By 1949, Issaquena County — well-known for its wildness, isolation and production of 10-point bucks — led the state in hunter numbers and deer harvested. An article in the January 1952 issue of *Mississippi Game and Fish*, titled "Camp and Wardens' Reports Indicate 3,000 Deer Killed in Mississippi," reported that Issaquena County hunters led the state by harvesting 360 deer during the November/December season. The harvest was achieved with 42 deer camps consisting of 1,389 hunters. In 1950, the Mississippi Legislature required all deer camp operators to acquire free permits from the Game and Fish Commission before setting up a camp.

Ten Point Deer Club member Billy Carter characterized the habitat surrounding the camp as a "cathedral-type place." In describing the haunting isolation where his grandfather Paul, the club's founder, chased 10-point bucks with gusto, Alan Huffman noted the county lacked incorporated towns:

"Aside from a few plantations near the Mississippi River, there was no real development. It was a place where hunters might prove their prowess in the woods, enjoy the camaraderie of a small circle of friends in an uncontested domain, and temporarily shed those conventions of civilized life that seem unnecessary there. In truncated form, these are still the primary attractions at deer camps today."

Camaraderie and socializing became the primary attractions at the Ten Point Deer Club. People didn't go there for deer meat. They went to have a good time, horse around and commune with nature. Deer hunting was not only a favorite recreation, but a time-honored social function to enjoy with family and friends. The camp became a continuation of a neighborhood way of life, and deer hunting emerged as a lifelong interest for club members.

At the end of the day, familiar voices told well-worn deer-hunting tales by the fire, with the sweet taste of whiskey polishing cherished yarns. The added shine, however, sometimes came at obvious expense of the facts, as reporter Jimmy Ward, a frequent observer of Ten Point, reported in the *Jackson Daily News*:

"After a hearty supper of sizzling 'deerburgers,' a culinary masterpiece originated by Dr. T.M. Moore, and venison chili — enough food for a lumberjack camp — the hunters recounted the day's hunt, some accounts couched in very false wording, statements issued for the truth but with facts twisted as subtly as a sledge hammer — in other words, some lying flowed across the board."

In 1939, this group incorporated under the name Ten Point Deer Club, and leased larger holdings from the Anderson-Tully Co. They now hunted deer on a tract of land ranging from 9,000 to 16,000 acres.

In 1941, they built an 18-by-60-foot clubhouse near the confluence of Steele Bayou and the Yazoo River. In the center of the clubhouse's main room, a large fire always roared in a barrel stove. Mounted 10-pointers and composites of photos of each deer hunt hung on the walls. The main bunk room housed as many as 30 hunters. According to Alan Huffman, the clubhouse became "a prominent landmark along the swampy bayou. ... Here, men who seldom cooked at home made a great ceremony of preparing meals that were long on meat, salt, lard, sugar and flour."

"The Clubhouse," Huffman continued, "gave an air of permanence to the Ten Point Deer Club, which until then had been nothing more than a loose confederation of hunters tramping the swamps in search of deer."

Deer stands surrounding Ten Point were all numbered or named — some after the club's legendary dogs, such as Rowdy and Bugle Ann. Each club member drew in a democratic manner for the best deer stands.

The membership of this old-school deer camp observed a time-honored ritual of deer hunting that goes back at least 10,000 years: smearing blood on the face of a hunter making his first kill. They also cut the shirttail from the hunter who missed his buck. The blood baptisms still occur in many deer camps today.

In his book, *Ten Point: Deer Camp in the Mississippi Delta*, Alan Huffman observed that

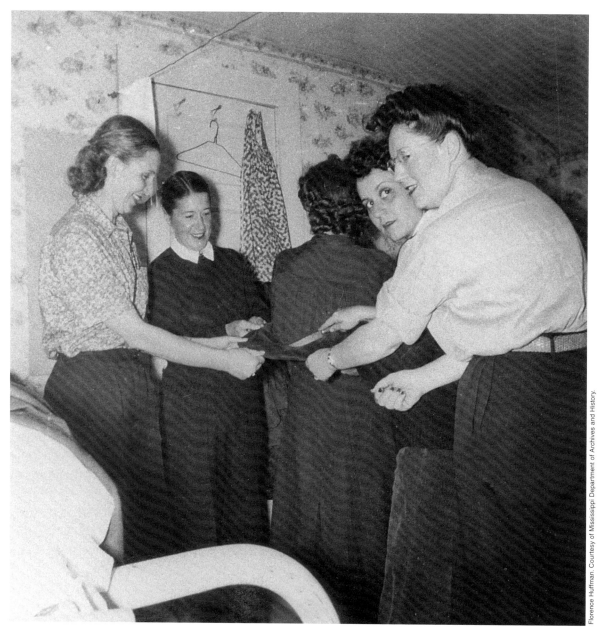

Florence Huffman. Courtesy of Mississippi Department of Archives and History.

Cutting a hunter's shirttail was a tradition after a missed shot. Above, four women cut the tail from Mama Florence's shirt. Right, other shirttails hang on the board.

"the personalities of the hunters come to the fore in Mama Florence's photos of the blood smearings, which involved taking a few handfuls of blood from the hunter's deer and smearing it upon his face. In some photos, another hunter gingerly applies the blood to the hunter's face; the preacher, Brother Johnston, was known for his gentle touch. In other photos, two or more hunters ganged up on the initiate, and the scene might be mistaken for a bloody wrestling match if not for the smiles on everyone's face. Often the hunters posed for Mama Florence afterward,

grinning through their mask of drying blood."

Behind this deer hunting ritual lies the belief that a boy becomes a man when he puts venison on the table. This ancient ritual also underscores the belief in the power and magic of blood itself; for blood is life itself. According to Leviticus 17:11, "the life of the flesh is in the blood." The blood of the deer represents the essence of a strong and virile life. When the young hunter is daubed with deer blood, he receives the strength, vigor and vitality to aid the survival of his deer hunting clan.

When the hunter misses an ideal meat shot, the huntmaster enacts the penalty for marksmanship unbefitting a model deer hunter: He cuts off the offender's shirttail, with the amount removed varying with the offense's severity. A hunter caught sleeping on his stand while a buck walks past or a hunter who suffers from buck fever might lose his entire shirt. While this deer camp ritual is done in a spirit of fun, the message is clear: The offenders' performance is below the group's standards and must improve.

The shirttail cutting ritual emerged as a castration substitute that Southern deer hunters derived from American Indian culture. The shirttails sometimes were hung on the clubhouse walls. At other times they were hung on a makeshift flagpole outside of the clubhouse to blow in the breeze for years, or even sent home to the hunter's wife for the ultimate in humiliation.

While Ten Point was primarily a male-dominated camp, the presence of so many female deer hunters made the camp unusual. Although they did not vote or reside as official members, women participated in the hunts, and photos of them with their deer appeared in Mama Florence's albums and journals. They also lost their shirttails when they missed a buck.

Issues of *Mississippi Game and Fish* — at that time published by the Mississippi Game and Fish Commission — included stories and photos of the Delta's female deer hunters. Photos of female hunters with bucks they shot also appeared on the magazine's cover occasionally, a phenomenon that never occurs today with magazines published by state wildlife agencies. Yet, despite the long-standing involvement of women at Ten Point, women were an aberration at traditionally male-oriented deer camps nationwide.

In 1940, the Ten Point Deer Club split into two groups because of inter-generational conflicts over such issues as dog-hunting vs. still-hunting, and shotguns vs. rifles. The Vicksburg faction maintained the lease's west-

Florence Huffman. Courtesy of Mississippi Department of Archives and History.

ern portion and created the Buckhorn Hunting Club. The deer hunters from Jackson retained the name Ten Point Deer Club and hunted the eastern territory.

In 1950, the two clubs formed the Ten Buck Conservation Association, an organization to hold leases, carry insurance policies against damage and liability claims, and provide an overall wildlife management plan. On April 1, 1950, the Ten Buck Conservation Association secured a 20-year deer hunting lease from the Anderson-Tully Co. for $1 — the first lease of its kind for the company. Both clubs, however, maintained their own hunting activities, rules and regulations.

In 1952, Florence and Paul Huffman moved to Ten Point's rustic clubhouse to become year-round residents. They lived there until 1963, when they sold the clubhouse and surrounding land under threat of condemnation by the federal government. In 1978, a reincarnation of the Ten Point Hunting Club and Buckhorn Hunting Club formed the Mahannah Deer Management Association to better manage wildlife populations. By 1987, the Mahannah Association comprised 26 deer hunting clubs

that encompassed 30,000 acres. It eventually became a case study in the trial and error experiences of deer biologists administering a Cooperative Deer Management Assistance Program, or DMAP, on private lands in Mississippi, and exists today as a Mississippi Wildlife Management Area.

Under the popular DMAP program, the deer biologist became a leader, motivator, educator and problem-solver for deer clubs. Law enforcement improved, as did landowner and hunter cooperation. The deer herd responded to harvest strategies, and crop-damage conflicts were resolved. The deer biologists' credibility, as viewed by hunters, also improved. Obviously, the Ten Point Deer Club played a significant role in creating a successful partnership with Mississippi deer hunting clubs and the Delta's overall deer-management programs.

Today, according to Jim Lipe Sr., a Ten Point director, "the clubs continue their long-standing tradition and look forward to many future years of enjoyment in the Eagle Lake area. The clubs' goal will continue to be one of good sportsmanship, sound wildlife management, and conservation of wildlife and natural resources." It now operates under the guidelines of quality deer management.

Hunters raised as adolescents in deer camps such as Ten Point have experienced it as a sacred place, and as sacred space. When they stand near the deer shack, they witness a startling and dramatic moment when the mind sees more deeply. They experience the possibility of something bigger going on, of something more significant than ourselves. As a result, they return to wilderness deer camps to experience this empowering sense of encounter. During such moments, they experience the ultimate reverence for the quarry and the cosmic significance of the chase.

The chase is transcendent. When man and

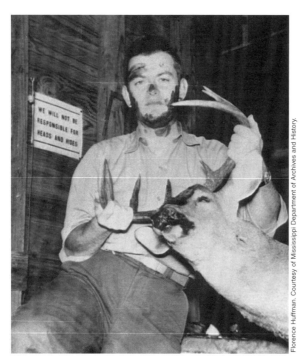

Florence Huffman. Courtesy of Mississippi Department of Archives and History.

This hunter practices the time-honored tradition of smearing blood on his face after his first kill.

Chip Cooper.

The Mississippi Delta has a colorful deer-hunting history that traditionally takes place in a highly spirited atmosphere of camaraderie.

the whitetail die, Faulkner wrote, they're free to do what they love most: participate in a mythical deer hunt in the sky, in "the long challenge and the long chase."

The ritual of deer hunting for many Ten Point members reaches it highest level when it becomes an initiation rite — a holy occupation ultimately played out in sacred space.

When today's deer hunters think of the original Ten Point Deer Club — a remote gathering place in the Delta wilderness for more than a half-century — they think of mud, mosquitoes, ticks and snakes; the Yazoo River ferry and the wharf on Steele Bayou; of cut shirttails, blood-smeared faces, and 10-point bucks pursued by panting horses and clamoring deer hounds.

We see the black-and-white deer hunting photos taken by Mama Florence, and swampy forests, rivers, lakes and bayous, cotton fields, catfish and virgin cypress trees. We also see men in long underwear telling tales in front of a big wood stove, Model T Fords on the Delta's flatlands and, as Alan Huffman notes, "iron beds lined up along the wall of the barracks-like bunk room."

We also relive the destruction and declining wilderness of the Delta and the devastation of World War II.

Ultimately, we think of the famous chili suppers at Ten Point, laced high-top leather boots, the campfire's flickering light, the sound and smell of sizzling venison tenderloins, the sweet taste of Southern whiskey, and the return to civilization while smelling like mud, gun oil and wood smoke.

POSTSCRIPT

As a European by cultural origin, I am struck again and again by both the richness of American culture — and by the ignorance surrounding it. Not only are North America's remarkable achievements in wildlife and nature conservation a well-kept secret here and abroad, so is — Walden Pond not withstanding — its romantic writings about man's deep and ultimate involvement with nature. This shallow, less-than-ultimate involvement views nature akin to art, as a Platonic love affair, of view-but-do-not-touch, as the "let it be" movement.

Wilderness assumes a cloak of sacredness, while man is viewed as the ultimate evil befallen Mother Earth. As much as one can have sympathy with this outlook in view of the enormous destruction inflicted currently on the biosphere by burgeoning masses of humanity and ruthless economics, it is neither a wholesome nor holistic outlook, nor one conducive to the repair of the biosphere. It might be a view supportive of national parks as icons, but not as a guide to our conduct on the vast land surfaces outside of national parks. No philosophy — if one can call it such — of self-hate can do that. Curing environmental ills requires not a stance outside nature, but a stance within nature, a role not as onlooker without, but as an actor within.

Ironically, how to be such an actor has been deeply thought about, lived and recorded by saints of the environmental movement, of wildlife conservation and of American folk literature, illustrated respectively in the preceding chapters by Aldo Leopold, Theodore Roosevelt, William Faulkner and others. Yes, saints, for the fruitful lives of these individuals led to more than widespread populist policies. They led to deep-rooted tangibles, such as the return of wildlife and the maintenance of biodiversity on this continent. Theses support the high quality of life in North America, while wildlife conservation American style is teeming with lessons for the future, for how to manage renewable resources in a sustainable manner, and how to restore Earth's biota.

Legendary Deer Camps brings to the fore the outlook on life as cherished by those who set in motion the great restoration of North America's wildlife in the 20th century. These healers and saints were hunters. Their passions reflect the universal drama of the hunt, enriched in America by its great ethnic mix, native people included. We read of a full-blooded romance with nature, yet one uniquely American. This is due in part to the high value we place on the worthiness of the individual and on our culture of personal freedom, and in part due to the biological uniqueness of American deer.

Deer camps are not European, no matter how much America's culture has its roots in the Old World. Deer camps can arise only where we are free to associate, free to talk, free to pursue happiness and free to responsibly bear arms. Deer camps are not restricted to an elite of wealth or power, deer camps form from peers that cover the spectrum of wealth and power in North America. Deer camps would be impossible without Americans cherishing the great public good of wildlife and of land held in common, or being willing to share privately held lands for hunting.

Without these arch-American policies, there would be no deer camps, but hunts by royalty, no matter in what disguise. Royal hunts would share the passion and fellowship typical of deer camps, but never its constructive democracy and the actions flowing therefrom, to link common people's passion to wildlife and its living space. Royal hunts have historically had the opposite effect: dividing people from wildlife, making the common folks hate wildlife with a passion.

However, deer camps would not exist without the uniqueness of American deer, the white-tailed deer in particular. Deer camps could not be based on red deer, which culturally is the European "deer-equivalent" of our whitetails. The democracy of the deer camp matches the chances of encountering and bagging the best of bucks. A 12-year-old Faulkner could bag The Great Buck, a feat so many senior fellow hunters aspired to. Deer hunts of European nobility divided deer by antler quality, with the most noble stags going to hunters of highest rank, a virtual impossibility to achieve with white-tailed bucks. Red deer are hunted in open landscapes, are usually naturally congregated, and if not, foresters in the service of nobility saw to it that they were for the benefit of their noble masters and guests. Gregarious deer in the open allow selectivity, but the hunting of shy hiders such as whitetails does not. Deer camps are thus uniquely American by the nature of North American culture and the nature of North American deer.

It is the great achievement of Dr. Robert Wegner to have winnowed these historical events and to bring the best of them so vividly to the attention of a broad American readership. Here is something Americans can be immensely proud of. Rob Wegner shows there is a rich romantic involvement in North America with the hunt, a contrast to the macho hunts of Hemingway fame. These have had a larger profile, which this book redresses. It also reveals to us the philosophies and mind-set of those who did do much to restore and protect North America's wildlife after the devastations of the 19th century.

And that's why this is so important a book, let alone an enjoyable one, pregnant with insights.

— *Valerius Geist, Ph.D.,*
professor emeritus of environmental science,
The University of Calgary.

References

Chapter 1

"Adventure of Solomon Sweatland, The." *History of Ashtabula County, Ohio*. Philadelphia: Williams Brothers, 1878. pp. 158-159.

Bohley, Lou. "The Great Hinckley Hunt." *Ohio Conservation Bulletin* 18(10), 1954. pp. 11+.

Cole, Harry Ellsworth. *Stagecoach and Tavern Tales of the Old Northwest*. Illinois: Southern Illinois University Press, 1997. 376 pp.

Cross, David W. "A Deer Hunt in Ohio." *Forest and Stream* 18(4): Feb. 23, 1882. pp. 67-68.

_____. "My Last Deer Hunt in Ohio." *Forest and Stream* 20(12): April 19, 1883. pp. 225-226.

Edwards, Samuel E. *The Ohio Hunter: Or a Brief Sketch of the Frontier Life of Samuel E. Edwards, the Great Bear and Deer Hunter of the State of Ohio*. Michigan: Review and Herald Stream Press, 1866. 240 pp.

History of Medina County. Chicago: Baskin & Battey, 1881. pp. 607-611.

Laycock, George. "Bucking the Waves." *The Hunters and the Hunted*. New York: Outdoor Life Books, 1990. pp. 52-60.

Perry, Oliver Hazard. *Hunting Expeditions of Oliver Hazard Perry of Cleveland Verbatim From His Diaries*. Ohio: Privately printed, 1899. 246 pp.

_____. *Hunting Expeditions of Oliver Hazard Perry*. Edited with an Introduction by John E. Howard. Wisconsin: St. Hubert's Press, 1994. 299 pp.

_____. ("Old Stout"). "Deer Hunt in Henry County, Ohio." *Spirit of the Times*. April 12, 1851. p. 91.

Pierce, Milton P. "Another Deer Hunt in Ohio." *Forest and Stream* 18(7): March 16, 1882. pp. 129-130.

Rice, Harvey. *Pioneers of the Western Reserve*. Boston: Lee and Sheppard, 1883. pp. 190-196.

Scrope, William. *The Art of Deer-Stalking*. London: John Murray, 1838. 436 pp.

Sterling, Dr. Elisha. "A Camp on the Cass." *Forest and Stream* 28(8): March 17, 1887. p. 156.

Street, Alfred Billings. *The Poems of Alfred B. Street*. New York: Clark & Austin, 1874. 319 pp.

Wegner, Robert. *Wegner's Bibliography on Deer and Deer Hunting*. Wisconsin: St. Hubert's Press, 1992. 328 pp.

Chapter 2

Bartlett, Ilo H. *Whitetails: Presenting Michigan's Deer Problem*. Michigan: Department of Conservation, 1938. 64 pp.

_____. *Michigan Deer*. Michigan: Department of Conservation, 1950. 50 pp.

Bennett, C. L., Jr., L. A. Ryel & L. J. Hawn. *A History of Michigan Deer Hunting*. Michigan: Department of Conservation, 1966. Research and Development Report #85. 66 pp.

Brompton, John J. "Our Seventeenth Annual Deer Hunt." *The Chicago Field*. 6(24): 386. Jan. 27, 1877.

_____. "Camp Life Memories. — Deer Hunting on the Snow." *The Chicago Field*. 7(12): 187. May 5, 1877. Part VII.

_____. "Camp Life Memories — Turkey Frank Slays the Monarch of the Glen." *The Chicago Field*. 7(13): 218. May 19, 1877. Part VIII.

Caton, John Dean. *The Antelope and Deer of America*. New York: Forest and Stream, 1877. 426 pp.

"Greenhorn." "Deer Hunting in Michigan. Part I." *Forest and Stream*. 7(14): 369-370. Jan. 18, 1877.

Laffin, W. Mackay. *Scribner's Monthly*. April, 1878. 15(6): 753-768. Reprinted in Alfred M. Mayer (editor), *Sport with Gun and Rod in American Woods and Waters*. London: F. Warne & Company, 1883. pp. 233-255.

Nichols, Edwin C. "A Sketch of the Nichols Deer Hunting Camps." In William B. Mershon, *Recollections of My Fifty Years of Hunting and Fishing*. Boston: The Stratford Co., 1923. pp. 89-97.

Petersen, Eugene T. *Hunters' Heritage: A History of Hunting in Michigan*. Michigan: Michigan United Conservation Clubs, 1979. 54 pp.

_____. *The History of Wild Life Conservation in Michigan, 1859-1921*. University of Michigan. Ph. D. Dissertation, 1952. 335 pp.

Wegner, Robert. *Wegner's Bibliography on Deer & Deer Hunting*. Wisconsin: St. Hubert's Press, 1992. 322 pp.

_____. "Deer & Deer Hunting, 1873: Lessons for the Future." *Deer & Deer Hunting*. 23(6): 25-29. January 2000.

Chapter 3

Bartlett, Ilo H. *Whitetails: Presenting Michigan's Deer Problem.* Michigan: Department of Conservation, 1938. 64 pp.

_____. *Michigan Deer.* Michigan: Department of Conservation, 1950. 50 pp.

Bennett, C. L., Jr., L. A. Ryel, and L. J. Hawn. *A History of Michigan Deer Hunting.* Michigan: Department of Conservation, 1966. Research and Development Report #85. 66 pp.

Lowe, Kenneth S. "Shiras: Sportsman Nonpareil." *Michigan Out-of-Doors.* February 1977. pp. 40-41.

Petersen, Eugene T. *Hunters' Heritage: A History of Hunting in Michigan.* Michigan. Michigan United Conservation clubs, 1979. 54 pp.

_____. *The History of Wildlife Conservation in Michigan, 1859-1921.* University of Michigan. Ph. D. Dissertation, 1952. 335 pp.

Reynolds, Phyllis R. "George Shiras III." Unpublished paper presented at the Marquette County Historical Society. Marquette, Michigan. Oct. 25, 1966.

Sajna, Mike. "George Shiras III: Father of Wildlife Photography." *Michigan Natural Resources.* November/December 1990. 59(6): 4-13.

Shiras, George III. *Hunting Wildlife with Camera and Flashlight.* Washington D. C.: The National Geographic Society, 1939. Two Volumes.

_____. *The Shiras Papers.* The Marquette County Historical Society, Inc. The J. M. Longyear Research Library. Marquette, Michigan.

_____. "Hunting with a Camera." *New York Sun.* Aug. 25, 1895. p. 12

Smith, Richard P. *Michigan Big Game Records.* Michigan: Commemorative Bucks of Michigan, Inc., 1986/1989/1993. Three editions.

Wegner, Robert. *Wegner's Bibliography on Deer & Deer Hunting.* Wisconsin: St. Hubert's Press, 1992. 322 pp.

Chapter 4

Collins, Michael L. *That Damned Cowboy: Theodore Roosevelt and the American West, 1883-1898.* New York: Peter Lang, 1989. 227 pp.

Knue, Joseph. *Big Game in North Dakota: A Short History.* North Dakota: North Dakota Game and Fish Department, 1991. 343 pp.

McGaffey, Ernest. "The Twelve-Tined Buck." *Poems of Gun and Rod.* New York: Charles Scribner's Sons, 1892. pp. 75-80.

McLellan, Isaac. "Deer Hunting in Maine." *Poems of the Rod and Gun.* New York: Henry Thorpe, 1886. pp. 37-39.

Morris, Edmund. *The Rise of Theodore Roosevelt.* New York: Ballantine Books, 1979. 886 pp.

Roosevelt, Theodore. "Shooting Near the Ranch-House — The Whitetail Deer." *The Works of Theodore Roosevelt.* Memorial edition. Vol. 1. New York: Charles Scribner's & Sons, 1923. pp. 320-328.

_____. "The Deer of the Upland and the Broken Ground." Ibid. pp. 329-335.

_____. "A Christmas Buck." *Good Hunting in Pursuit of Big Game in the West.* New York: Harper & Brothers, Publishers, 1907. pp. 351-372.

_____. "The Ranchman's Rifle on Crag and Prairie." *Ranch Life and the Hunting Trail.* Nebraska: University of Nebraska Press, I983. pp. 131-145. (First published in 1888).

_____. "The Whitetail Deer." *Outdoor Pastimes of an American Hunter.* New York: Charles Scribner's Sons, 1923. pp. 215-249. (First published in 1893).

_____. "The Mule-Deer or Rocky Mountain Blacktail." Ibid. pp. 250-285.

_____, et. al. *The Deer Family.* New York: The Macmillian Company, 1902. 334 pp.

_____. "The Black-Tail Deer." *Hunting Trips of a Ranchman.* South Carolina: The Premier Press, 1990. pp. 134-190. (First published in 1885.)

_____. "The Deer of the River Bottoms." Ibid. pp. 108-133.

_____. "Hunting from the Ranch: The Blacktail Deer." *The Wilderness Hunter.* South Carolina: The Premier Press, 1987, pp. 20-36. (First published in 1893.)

_____. "The Whitetail Deer; And the Blacktail of the Columbia." Ibid. pp. 37-54.

Schullery, Paul. (editor). *Theodore Roosevelt: Wilderness Writings.* Utah: Peregrine Smith Books, 1986. 292 pp.

Wegner, Robert. *Wegner's Bibliography on Deer and Deer Hunting.* Wisconsin: St. Hubert's Press, 1992. 322 pp.

Wilson, R. L. *Theodore Roosevelt: Outdoorsman.* New York: Winchester Press, 1971. 278 pp.

Chapter 5

Bersing, Otis. *A Century of Wisconsin Deer*. Wisconsin: Department of Conservation, 1966. 272 pp.

Cowley, Mert. *A Hundred Hunts Ago: Seasons of the Past*. Wisconsin: Privately printed, 1996. 519 pp.

Dahlberg, Burton L. and Ralph C. Guettinger. *The White-Tail Deer In Wisconsin*. Wisconsin: Department of Conservation, 1956. 282 pp.

Iron River Centennial, 1892-1992. Wisconsin: Privately printed, 1992. 231 pp.

Iron River Pioneer, 1880-1943. Wisconsin State Historical Society, Madison, Wisconsin.

Lund, Fred P. "Wigs". *I Mind: Memories of the Old Hunting Camp Days*. Minnesota: Privately printed, 1969. 78 pp.

_____. "Me, The Mighty Buckhunter." *Iron River: My Home Town*. Minnesota: Privately printed, 1975. pp. 14-29.

_____. "The Last of the Hunting Camp Days." *Iron River: My Home Town*. Minnesota: Privately printed, 1975. pp. 30-41.

_____. "Deer Hunting Episodes of Yesteryear." *And That's The Way It Was*. Minnesota: Privately printed, 1973. pp. 96-115.

_____. "My Father — The Game Warden." *And That's The Way It Was*. Minnesota: Privately printed, 1973. pp. 134-158.

_____. "The Big Drive." *Deer & Deer Hunting*. November/December 1983. (7)2: 74-80.

_____. "The Deer Hunter." *Deer & Deer Hunting*. November/December 1983. (7)2: 8-9.

Schorger, A. W. "The White-Tailed Deer in Early Wisconsin." Transactions of the Wisconsin Academy of Sciences. 42(1953): 197-247.

Swift, Ernest. *A History of Wisconsin Deer*. Wisconsin: Department of Conservation, 1946. 96 pp.

Wegner, Robert. *Wegner's Bibliography on Deer & Deer Hunting*. *Wisconsin*: St. Hubert's Press, 1992. 328 pp.

_____. "A Legendary Wisconsin Whitetail." *Wisconsin Outdoor Journal*. Hunting Annual 1996. 10(7): 32-34.

_____. "The Homer Pearson Buck." *Quality Whitetails*. Fall/Winter 1993/1994. pp. 18-20.

_____. "The Homer Pearson Buck." In *Legendary Whitetails*, edited by Gordon Whittington and David Morris. Montana: Venture Press, 1996. pp. 158-163.

Chapter 6

Bersing, Otis. *A Century of Wisconsin Deer*. Wisconsin: Wisconsin Department of Conservation, 1956. 272 pp.

Dahlberg, B.L. & R.C. Guettinger. *The White-tailed Deer in Wisconsin*. Wisconsin: Wisconsin Department of Conservation, 1956. 279 pp.

Freund, Win. "Deerfoot Lodge." *The Daily Herald*. Dec. 3, 1981. pp. 10-11. Wausau, Wisconsin.

Jackson, Robert, & Robert Norton. "Deer Hunting is a Family Affair." *Wisconsin Natural Resources*. November/December 1979. pp. 10-15.

Rosenberry, M.B. *A History of Deerfoot Lodge: Memories of Happy Hunting*. Wisconsin: Privately printed, 1941. 70 pp.

_____. Unpublished Papers. State Historical Society of Wisconsin.

Swift, Ernest. *A History of Wisconsin Deer*. Wisconsin: Wisconsin Department of Conservation, 1946. 96 pp.

Tenney, Horace Kent. *Vert & Venison*. Chicago: Privately printed, 1924. 153 pp.

Wegner, Robert. *Wegner's Bibliography on Deer & Deer Hunting*. Wisconsin: St. Hubert's Press, 1992. 328 pp.

Wisconsin Trophy Records. Wisconsin: Buck & Bear Club, 1994. 139 pp.

Chapter 7

Ashley, Steve. (ed.) *Wisconsin Trophy Records*. Wisconsin: Wisconsin Buck & Bear Club, 1994. Volume 5. 139 pp.

Bersing, Otis. *A Century of Wisconsin Deer*. Wisconsin: Department of Conservation, 1956. 272 pp.

Cowley, Mert. (ed.) *A Hundred Hunts Ago: Seasons of the Past*. Wisconsin: Privately Printed, 2000. Revised edition. 519 pp.

Dahlberg, B.L. and R.C. Guettinger. *The White-Tailed Deer in Wisconsin*. Wisconsin: Department of Conservation, 1946. 282 pp.

LaBarbera, Mark. (ed.) *Wisconsin Deer & Bear Record Book*. Minnesota: Privately printed, 1984. 248 pp.

Ladysmith News. 1916-1928. State Historical Society of Wisconsin.

Ladysmith News. "The Bucks Camp Members and Guests Killed 10 Deer." Nov. 30, 1917.

Swift, Ernest. *History of Wisconsin Deer*. Wisconsin: Department of Conservation, 1946. 96 pp.

Terrill, John. "Terrills' Tails, Trails & Tales." *The Ladysmith News.* Thursday, Nov. 8, 1979. Section C.

_____. "Terrills' Tails, Trails & Tales." *The Ladysmith News.* Thursday, Nov. 5, 1981. p. 9B.

Wegner, Robert. *Wegner's Bibliography on Deer & Deer Hunting.* Wisconsin: St. Hubert's Press, 1992. 328 pp.

Williams, Marjorie. (ed.) *The Bucks Camp Log, 1916-1928.* Wisconsin: Wisconsin Sportsman, 1974. 111 pp.

_____. *The Bucks Camp Log*, 1916-1928. Wisconsin: Willow Creek Press, 1989 Second edition. 105 pp.

Wisconsin Department of Conservation. Biennial Report of the Conservation Department for 1921-1922. Madison, Wis.

Chapter 8

Bersing, Otis. *Bow and Arrow Big Game Hunting in Wisconsin.* Wisconsin: Privately printed, 1973. 272 pp.

_____. *Fifteen Years of Bow and Arrow Deer Hunting in Wisconsin.* Wisconsin: Department of Conservation, 1949. 24 pp.

Callicott, J. Baird. *In Defense of the Land Ethic.* New York: State University of New York Press, 1989. 325 pp.

Elder, John. "Hunting in Sand County." *Orion: Nature Quarterly.* Autumn 1986. pp. 46-53.

Flader, Susan. *Thinking Like a Mountain: Aldo Leopold and the Evolution of an Ecological Attitude Toward Deer, Wolves and Forests.* Missouri: University of Missouri Press, 1974. 284 pp.

Leopold, Aldo. *The Leopold Papers.* University of Wisconsin Archives — Madison.

_____. *Round River: From the Journals of Aldo Leopold.* New York: Oxford University Press, 1953. 173 pp.

_____. *A Sand County Almanac and Sketches Here and There.* New York: Oxford University Press, 1987. 269 pp.

McCabe, Robert A. "As a Hunter." *Aldo Leopold: The Professor.* Wisconsin: University of Wisconsin Press, 1988. pp. 124-128.

McCullough, Dale. "North American Deer Ecology: Fifty Years Later." *In Aldo Leopold: The Man and His Legacy* edited by Thomas Tanner. Iowa: Soil Conservation Society of America, 1987. pp. 115-122.

Meine, Curt. *Aldo Leopold: His Life and Work. Wisconsin:* University

of Wisconsin Press, 1988. 638 pp.

_____, and Richard L. Knight. (eds.) *Essential Aldo Leopold: Quotations and Commentaries.* UW Press, 1999. 384 pp.

Wegner, Robert. *Wegner's Bibliography on Deer and Deer Hunting.* Wisconsin: St. Hubert's Press, 1992. 328 pp.

Chapter 9

Altherr, Thomas L. "The Best of all Breathing: The Wilderness Career of Isaac McCaslin in William Faulkner's The Old People, The Bear and Delta Autumn." *Cynegeticus: A Publication Devoted to the Interdisciplinary Study of Hunting.* 5(3): 1-11. July 1981.

Blotner, Joseph. *Faulkner: A Biography.* New York: Random House, 1974. 778 pp.

Bradford, M. E. "The Winding Horn: Hunting and the Making of Men in Faulkner's 'Race at Morning.'" *Papers on English Language & Literatur*e. 1(1): 272-278. Winter 1965.

Brite, Jerrold. "A True-Blue Hunter." In *William Faulkner of Oxford.* Edited by James W. Webb and A. Wigfall Green. Louisiana: Louisiana State University Press, 1965. pp. 154-161.

Cullen, John B. "Faulkner in a Hunter's Camp." *Old Times in the Faulkner Country.* Louisiana: Louisiana State University Press, 1961. pp12-17.

Faulkner Journal. Ada, Ohio. 1985 - The Present.

Faulkner, William. "The Old People." Harper's Magazine. September 1940. Volume 181. pp. 418-425.

_____. *Big Woods: The Hunting Stories of William Faulkner.* New York: Random House, 1955. 198 pp.

Faulkner, John. *My Brother Bill: An Affectionate Reminiscence.* New York: Trident Press, 1963. 277 pp.

Hamblin, Robert W., and Charles A. Peek. (ed.) *A William Faulkner Encyclopedia.* Connecticut: Greenwood Press, 1999. 490 pp.

Hoffman, Daniel. *Faulkner's Country Matters.* Louisiana: Louisiana State University Press, 1989. 181 pp.

Holmes, Rolston III. "Hunting." *Environmental Ethics: Duties to and Values in the Natural World.* Philadelphia: Temple University Press, 1988. pp. 88-93.

Karl, Frederick R. *William Faulkner: An American Writer.* New York: Ballantine Books, 1989. 1,131 pp.

Kinney, Arthur F. *Go Down, Moses: The Miscegenation of Time.* New York: Twayne Publishers, 1996. 181 pp

McHaney, Thomas L. "A Deer Hunt in the Faulkner Country." *Mississippi Quarterly*. Summer, 1970. pp. 315-320.

Marks, Stuart A. *Southern Hunting in Black and White: Nature, History and Ritual in a Carolina Community*. New Jersey: Princeton University Press, 1991. 327 pp.

Messenger, Christian K. *Sport and the Spirit of Play in Contemporary American Fiction*. New York: Columbia University Press, 1990. 473 pp.

"Mississippi Deer Hunters Have Best Year In 1949." *Mississippi Game and Fish*. 13(7): Jan. 3, 1959.

Oates, Stephen B. *William Faulkner: The Man and the Artist*. New York: Harper & Row, Publishers, 1987. 363 pp.

Pittman, Barbara L. "Faulkner's Big Woods and the Historical Necessity of Revision." *Mississippi Quarterly*. 49(3): 475-495. Summer 1996.

Prewitt, Wiley C. Jr. "Return of the Big Woods: Hunting and Habitat in Yoknapatawpha." In *Faulkner and the Natural World*, edited by Donald M. Kartiganer and Ann J. Abodie. Mississippi: University of Mississippi, 1999. pp. 198-221.

Oxford Eagle. 1900-1962.

Rash, Ron. "Do You Write, Mr. Faulkner?" *Sporting Classics*, 4(1): 18-23, 68-71. March/April 1985.

Ruzicka, William T. "Go Down, Moses." *Faulkner's Fictive Architecture: The Meaning of Place in the Yoknapatawpha Novels*. Michigan: UMI Research Press, 1987. pp. 83-110.

Veblen, Thorstein. *The Theory of the Leisure Class*. New York: B. W. Huebsch, 1924, 404 pp.

Wegner, Robert. *Wegner's Bibliography on Deer and Deer Hunting*. Wisconsin: St. Hubert's Press, 1992. 328 pp.

Wittenberg, Judith Byrant. "Go Down, Moses and the Discourse of Environmentalism." In *New Essays on Go Down Moses*. Edited by Linda Wagner-Martin. New York: Cambridge University Press, 1996. pp. 49-71.

Chapter 10

Bersing, Otis. *A Century of Wisconsin Deer*. Wisconsin: Department of Conservation, 1966. 272 pp.

Dahlberg, Burton L. and Ralph C. Guettinger. *The White-Tailed Deer in Wisconsin*. Wisconsin: Wisconsin Conservation Department, 1956. 282 pp.

Ellis, Mel. "Life in Wisconsin's Old-Time Deer Camps." In Sue McCoy (ed.) *Yarns of Wisconsin*. Wisconsin: Tamarack Press, 1978. pp. 168-172.

Gottschalk, Gordon. *History of Buckshot, Incorporated, 1956-1986*. Wisconsin: Privately printed, n. d. 64 pp.

_____. Unpublished letter to Robert Wegner. Feb. 5, 1993.

_____. Unpublished letter to Robert Wegner. Jan. 12, 1993.

Heberlein, Thomas. *Wisconsin Deer Hunter Survey*. Wisconsin: University of Wisconsin, 1981.

Jackson, Robert M. "Hunting as a Social Experience." *Deer & Deer Hunting*. 11(2): 38-51. 1987.

Lake Mills Leader, The. "Seven Bag Deer At Wollin Game Lodge Near Cable." Nov. 29, 1956.

_____. "All Hunters At Cable Lodge Got Deer." Dec. 1, 1949.

_____. "Hunters Get Trophies." Dec. 2, 1948.

_____. "Hunters Return From North With Much Venison." Dec. 2, 1943.

_____. "Seven Deer Killed At Sharp-Wollin Lodge Near Cable." Dec. 3, 1947.

MacQuarrie, Gordon. "You've Got to Suffer." *Stories of the Old Duck Hunters and Other Drivel*. Pennsylvania: Stackpole Books, 1967. pp. 149-158.

Stinker, Major I. M. A. *Citation or Ode to Combs*. Wisconsin: High Committee on Skullduggery, Nov. 9, 1958.

Varney, V. V. "O. B. Shot a Bear." Unpublished essay in Buckshot Inc., Record Book, 1928—.

Wegner, Robert. Wegner's *Bibliography on Deer and Deer Hunting*. Wisconsin: St. Hubert's Press, 1992. 328 pp.

Wileden, Arthur F. *The Buckshot Story, 1928-1972*. Wisconsin: Privately printed, n.d. 20 pp.

_____. "Wisconsin Whitetails." *A Lifetime of Hunting and Fishing Experiences*. Wisconsin: Privately printed, 1982. pp. 94-102.

_____. "Whitetails I Have Missed." *A Lifetime of Hunting and Fishing Experiences*. Wisconsin: Privately printed, 1982. pp. 103-117.

Wollin, A. C. Sr. "Reports on Deer Hunting in the Area near Cable." *The Lake Mills Leader*, Lake Mills, Wisconsin. 12-17-53.

_____. "Deer Season Poorest In Many Years — Reports A. C. Wollin." *The Lake Mills Leader*. Dec. 4, 1952.

"Wollin Game Lodge Registers A Top Year of Hunting." *The Lake Mills Leader*. Lake Mills,Wisconsin. Newspaper clipping without date.

Chapter 11

Abernethy, Francis E. "The East Texas Communal Hunt." In *Hunters & Healers: Folklore Types & Topics*. Edited by Wilson M. Hudson. Texas: The Encino Press, 1971. Pages 3-10.

Birdshot. "Deer Hunting in Mississippi." *Forest and Stream*. May 4, 1907. 68(18): 697.

Boone. "Deer Hunting in Mississippi." *Spirit of the Times*. Nov. 19, 1842. 12(38): 445.

Boykin, Henry D. II. *Looking Back At The Boykin Hunting Club*. South Carolina: Privately printed, 1984. 128 pages.

Bullock, Jimmy. "Hunting Clubs and Deer Management: Keys to a Successful Partnership." *Quality Whitetails*. 2(2): 13-15, 19, 27. 1995.

"Camp and Wardens' Reports Indicate 3000 Deer Killed in Mississippi." *Mississippi Game and Fish*. XV(7): 8-9. January 1952.

C. H. "The Horn of the Hunter: On the Banks of the Yazoo." *Forest and Stream*. Jan. 6, 1900. Volume 54. p. 2.

Faulkner, William. "Delta Autumn." *Story Magazine*. Volume 20. May/June 1942. pp. 46-55.

Gohdes, Clarence. (ed.) *Hunting in the Old South: Original Narratives of the Hunters*. Louisiana: Louisiana State University Press, 1967. 176 pp.

G. W. P. "Deer Hunting in Mississippi." *Spirit of the Times*. March 13, 1858. 28(5): 56.

Herbert, Henry William. ("Frank Forester.") *Frank Forester's Field Sports of the United States and British Provinces of North America*. New York: N. A. Townsend & Company, 1860. Two volumes.

Huffman, Alan. *Ten Point: Deer Camp in the Mississippi Delta*. Mississippi: University Press of Mississippi, 1997. 134 pages.

Ingraham, Joseph Holt. "A Natchez Deer Hunt." *In The South-West. By A Yankee*. New York: Harper & Brothers, 1835. Volume 1. Pp. 132-139.

Lamar, May and Rich Donnell. *Hunting: The Southern Tradition*. Texas: Taylor Publishing Company, 1987. 198 pages.

Leopold, Aldo. *Report on a Game Survey of Mississippi*. Feb. 1, 1929.

Lipe, Jim Sr. and Bedford Jacks. "Ten Point & Buckhorn Hunting Clubs." *The Habitat*. April 1989. 6(1): 16.

McDonald, J. Scott and Karl V. Miller. *A History of White-Tailed Deer Restocking in the United States, 1818-1992*. South Carolina: A Publication of The Quality Deer Management Association, 1993. 109 pp.

Marks, Stuart A. *Southern Hunting in Black and White: Nature, History, and Ritual in a Carolina Community*. New Jersey: Princeton University Press, 1991. 327 pp.

Noble, Robert E. "Mississippi's Deer Herd: Past and Present." *Mississippi Game & Fish*. November/December 1966. 25(6): 14-15.

Ownby, Ted. *Subduing Satan: Religion, Recreation, & Manhood in the Rural South, 1865-1920*. North Carolina: The University of North Carolina Press, 1990. 286 pp.

Prewitt, Wiley C. "Return of the Big Woods: Hunting and Habitat in Yoknapatanpha." In *Faulkner and the Natural World* edited by Donald M. Kartiganer and Ann J. Abodie. Mississippi: University Press of Mississippi, 1997. Pp. 198-221.

Shackelfork, Jacob Jr. "A Deer Hunt in Mississippi." *Spirit of the Times*. May 4, 1850. 20(11): 126.

Shepard, Paul. *Coming Home to the Pleistocene*. California: Island Press, 1998. 193 pp.

Sitton, Thad. *Backwoodsmen: Stockmen and Hunters along a Big Thicket River Valley*. Oklahoma: University of Oklahoma Press, 1995. 310 pp.

Ward, Jimmy. "Anything Can Happen Along The Winding Trail Of A Fast Buck." *Jackson (Miss.) Daily News*. Sunday, Jan. 4, 1953.

————. "A Deer Hunter May Sit For Days And Never See A Buck But He'll Be Back On The Stand Next Year." *Jackson (Miss.) Daily News*. Sunday, Jan. 3, 1954.

Wegner, Robert. "The Deer Club: The Wave of the Future." *Deer & Deer Hunting*. 15(3): 18, 20-30. October 1991.

Wood, C.H. "Deer and Turkey Shooting in Southern Mississippi." *The American Field*. July 29, 1893.

Yazoo. "Deer Hunting in the Yazoo Swamp." *Spirit of the Times*. 19(67): April 6, 1844.

Books

Anderson, Luther A. "The Deer Camp." *How to Hunt Whitetail Deer*. New York: Funk & Wagnalls, 1968. pp. 98-102.

Andrews, J. D., and Bill Molitor. "Profile of a Black Hills Deer Camp: The Sturm Camp." *Trophy Bucks of South Dakota*. South Dakota: Staghorn Mountain Publishing, 1989. pp. 215-218.

Back Then: A Pictorial History of Americans Afield. Wisconsin: Willow Creek Press, 1989.

Bass, Rick. *The Deer Pasture*. Texas: Texas A & M University Press, 1985.

Bauer, Erwin. "Your Hunting Camp on Wheels." *The Digest Book of Deer Hunting*. Chicago: Folett Publishing Company, 1979. pp. 31-35.

Benoit, Larry. *How to Bag the Biggest Buck of Your Life*. Vermont: Whitetail Press, 1974.

_____. *The Beginning: Where it All Began*. Vermont: Privately printed, 1992.

Bodes, Gerald W. *Organizing and Operating a Successful Hunting Club*. Illinois: Flyway Publishing Com., Inc., 1985.

Boykin, Henry D. *Looking Back at the Boykin Hunting Club*. South Carolina: Privately printed, 1984.

Bridges, Harry P. *The Woodmont Story*. New York: A. S. Barnes & Company, 1953.

Carter, Henry H. *Early History of the Santee Club*. South Carolina. Privately printed, 1904.

Cochran, Bruce. *Buck Fever: Deer Camp Cartoons*. Wisconsin: Willow Creek Press, 1990.

Cowley, Mert. *The Ultimate Stand: Poetic Tales of Deer Hunting from the Pearly Swamp Camp*. Wisconsin: Privately printed, 1990.

_____. *In Camps of Orange: Poetic Tales of Deer Hunting from the Pearly Swamp Camp*. Wisconsin: Privately printed, 1993.

_____. *A Hundred Hunts Ago: Seasons of the Past*. Wisconsin: Privately printed, 2000.

Christy, Bayard D. *The Book of Huron Mountain: A Collection of Papers Concerning the History of the Huron Mountain Club*. Michigan: The Huron Mountain Club, 1929.

Cook, Sam. "Deer Camp Characters." *Friendship Fires*. Minnesota: Pfeifer-Hamilton, 1999. pp. 98-102.

Davis, Richard E. *Deer Camp: Oswegatchie River and Other Places*. New York: Privately printed, 1996

Dickey, Charle. "All the Comforts of Deer Camp." *Movin' Along with Charley Dickey*. New Jersey: Winchester Press, 1985, pp. 57-62.

Ellis, Mel. "Life in Wisconsin's Old-Tme Deer Camps." In *Yarns of Wisconsin* edited by Sue McCoy. Wisconsin: Wisconsin Trails / Tamarack Press, 1978. pp. 168-172

Epler, E. P. "The Back Trackers One and Two." *80 Years in God's Country*. Illinois: Privately printed, 1973. pp. 108-115.

Franklin, Carlyle, Gerald Moore and Lewis Rogers. "Selective Harvesting of White-Tailed Buck Deer on Groton Plantation in South Carolina." In *Game Harvest Mangement* edited by Samuel L. Beasom and Sheila F. Robertson. Texas: Caesar Kleberg Wildlife Research Institute, 1985. pp. 175-183.

Grusendorf, Bill. "Women in Deer Camps." *Fifty Years of White-Tailed Deer Hunting*. New York: Vantage, 1961. pp. 66-68.

Hanks, Charles Stedman. *Camp Kits and Camp Life*. New York: Charles Scribner's Sons, 1906.

Huffman, Alan. *Ten Point: Deer Camp in the Mississippi Delta*. Mississippi: University Press of Mississippi, 1997.

Kilgo, James. *Deep Enough for Ivorybills*. North Carolina: Chapel Hill, 1988.

Koller, Larry. "The Deer Hunter's Camp." *Shots at Whitetails*. New York: Alfred A. Knopf, 1970. pp. 162-169.

Kozicky, Edward L. *Hunting Preserves for Sport or Profit*. Texas: Caesar Kleberg Wildlife Research Institute, 1987.

Kroll, James C. "Organizing a Hunting Club." *Producing and Harvesting White-Tailed Deer*. Texas: Stephen F. Austin State University, 1991. pp. 535-549.

Laffan, W. Mackay. "Deer Hunting on the Au Sable." In *Sport with Gun and Rod* edited by Alfred M. Mayer. New York: Century Company, 1883. pp. 233-256.

Lamar, May & Rich Donnell. *Hunting: The Southern Tradition*. Texas: Taylor Publishing Company, 1987.

Landers, Gunnard. *The Hunting Shack*. New York: Arbor House, 1979.

Leopold, Luna B. *Round River: From the Journals of Aldo Leopold*. New York: Oxford University Press, 1953.

Lott, Baret. *The Hunt Club: A Novel*. New York: Villard, 1998

Lund, Fred P. *I Mind*. Minnesota: Privately printed, 1969.

_____. *And That's the Way it Was*. Minnesota: Privately printed, 1973.

_____. *My Home Town*. Minnesota: Privately printed, 1975.

Madson, John. "Palace in the Popple." Reprinted in *The White-Tailed Deer*. Ilinois: Winchester Press, 1961. p. 3.

McLellan, Isaac. "Hunter's Camp at Night." *Poems of the Rod and Gun*. New York: Henry Thorpe, 1886. pp. 98-99.

McQueen, John D. *A Factual History of "Dollarhide." With Some Sidelights and Observations*. Alabama: Privatley printed, 1943.

Minehart, Charles D. *Meat on the Pole! A Story of the Orrstown Hunting Club, 1897-1947*. Pennsylvania: Privately printed, 1948.

Merrill, Lawrence "Pete." *Deer Trails and Camp Tales*. Michigan: Privately printed, 1983.

_____. *Logging Trails and a Sportsman's Tales*. Michigan: Privately printed, 1987.

Michmerhuizen, Lewey. *Grandpa Recalls Deer Hunting Stories*. Michigan: Privately printed, 1964.

Miller, John M. *Deer Camp: Last Light in the Northeast Kingdom*. Massachuetts: The MIT Press, 1992.

Milling, Chapman J. *Buckshot and Hounds*. New York: A. S. Barnes and Company, 1967.

Mitchell, John G. *The Hunt*. New York: Alfred A. Knopf, 1980.

Nachazel, Greg. *Deer Camp Dictionary: Hunting Terms of EnDEERment*. Michigan: Rhodes & Easton, 1997.

Nichols, Edwin C. "A Sketch of the Nichols Deer Hunting Camps." In *Recollections of my Fifty Years of Hunting and Fishing* by William B. Mershon. Boston: The Stratford Company, 1923. pp. 89-97.

Norris, Ralph S. "The Hunting Camp." *Science of Hunting the Whitetail Deer*. Maine: Privately printed, 1972. pp. 27-33.

Nugent, Ted. "Deercamp." *God, Guns, & Rock 'n' Roll*. Washington D. C.: Regnery Publishing Company, 2000. pp. 231-236.

O'Connor, David. "Deer Camp: Maine Hunting Tradition." In *The Maine Sportsman Book of Deer Hunting* edited by Harry Vanderweide. Maine: The Maine Sportsman, n. d. pp. 107-109.

Parrish, J. C. *Whitetails*. Detroit: Harlo, 1978.

Perry, Oliver Hazaard. *Hunting Expeditions of Oliver Hazard Perry of Cleveland*. Ohio: Privately printed, 1899.

Petersen, Eugene T. *Hunters' Heritage: A History of Hunting in Michigan*. Michigan: United Conservation Clubs, 1979.

Peterson, B. R. "Buck." *Buck Peterson's Complete Guide to Deer Hunting*. California: Ten Speed Press, 1989.

Phillips, John. C. "Camps." *A Sportsman's Scrapbook*. New York: Houghton Mifflin Company, 1929. pp. 13-51.

Potter, Arthur G., et. al. *The 1907 Hunt of the Forest City Hunting Club*. Cleveland: Privately printed, 1908.

Randolph, John. "Hawk Who Walks Hunting." In *Seasons of the Hunter* edited by Robert Elman and David Seybold. New York: Alfred A. Knopf, 1985. pp. 183-195.

Rau, Ed. Jr. *Wytopitloc: Tales of a Deer Hunter*. Maine: Dan River Press, 1999.

Rosenberry, M. B. *A History of Deerfoot Lodge: Memories of Happy Hunting*. Madison: Privately printed, 1908.

Roosevelt, Theodore. *Hunting Trips of a Ranchman*. South Carolina: The Premier Press, 1990.

_____. *The Wilderness Hunter*. S. Carolina: The Premier Press, 1987.

_____. *Ranch Life and the Hunting Trail*. Nebraska: University of Nebraska Press, 1983.

Sajna, Mike. *Buck Fever: The Deer Hunting Tradition in Pennsylvania*. Pennsylvania: University of Pittsburg Press, 1990.

Salley, A. S. Jr. *The Happy Hunting Ground*. South Carolina: Privately printed, 1926.

Shaffmaster, A. D. *Hunting in the Land of Hiawatha*. Illinois: M.A. Donohue & Company, 1904.

Streyckmans, Felix B. *The Story of Our Club*. Illinois: The Schori Press, 1968.

Tenney, Horace Kent. "The Cabin on the Bay." *Vert and Venison*. Chicago: Privately printed, 1924. p. 72.

Tiger, Lion. *Men in Groups*. New York: Random House, 1969.

Towsley, Bryce. *Big Bucks the Benoit Way: Secrets from America's First Family of Whitetail Hunting*. Wisconsin: Krause Publications, 1998.

Wegner, Robert. "Deer Camp." *Deer & Deer Hunting*. Harrisburg: Stackpole Books, 1984 pp. 182-195.

_____. "Deer Camps in the Land of Hiawatha." *Deer & Deer Hunting: Book 2*. Harrisburg: Stackpole Books, 1987. pp. 195-216.

_____. "The American Deer Camp." *Deer & Deer Hunting: Book 3*. Harrisburg: Stackpole Books, 1990. pp. 186-205.

_____. *Wegner's Bibliography on Deer & Deer Hunting*. Wisconsin: St. Hubert's Press, 1990.

Williams, Glenn H. *The Bucks Camp Log, 1916-1928*. Wisconsin: Wisconsin Sportsman, 1974.

Wolfe, Oliver Howard. *Back Log and Pine Knot: A Chronicle of the Minnisink Hunting and Fishing Club.* Philadelphia: Privately printed, 1916.

Journal, Magazine and Newspaper Articles

Abbott, Mrs. S. E. "Women in Camp." *Recreation.* June, 1898. 8(6): 449-451.

Apel, E. E. "Naming a Deer Hunting Camp." *Deer & Deer Hunting.* May/ June 1982. 5(5): 51-52

Alsheimer, Charles J. "Harmony in the Heart of Deer Country." *Deer & Deer Hunting.* November/December 1983. 7(2): 66-73

_____. "Legendary Adirondack Deer Camps." *Deer & Deer Hunting.* November, 1989. 13(3):12-20.

Atwill, Lionel. "Just One More: Lost Soul's Deer Camp." *Sports Afield.* November 1981. p. 164.

_____. "Deer Camp." *Field & Stream.* November 2000. pp. 57-64.

Barrett, Paul M. "The Old Hunting Camp." *Michigan Conservation.* November/December 1964. pp. 17-24.

Bashline, Jim. "The Great American Deer Camp." *Field & Stream.* November 1982. pp. 55+.

Blouch, Ralph I. "Winter Deer Mortality on Two Private Hunting Clubs." Papers of the Michigan Academy of Science, Arts and Letters, 1961. Volume 66. pp. 277-287.

Boitnott, Richard. "Following Rules Important for Clubs." *The Wood's Edge.* Fall, 1999. p. 2.

"Booze & Buckshort (Hurley, Wisconsin)." *Time.* Dec. 1, 1961. p. 54.

Bourne, Wade. "The Shack: A Hunting Legacy." *Alabama Game & Fish.* January 1981. pp. 14-16.

Bouwman, Fred. "Deer Camp Delicacies." *Deer & Deer Hunting.* November/December, 1981. 9(2): 84-89.

Bullock, Jimmy. "Hunting Clubs and Deer Management: Keys to a Successful Partnership." *Quality Whitetails.* 1995. 2(2): 13-15, 19, 27.

Busch, Frederick A. & David C. Guynn, Jr. "Characteristics of Deer Hunting Lessees in South Carolina and Mississippi." Proceedings of the Annual Conference of the Southeastern Association of Fish and Wildlife Agencies. 1987. 41: 266-270.

Chamberlaine, Lee. "The Deer Camp." *The Conservationist.* November/December, 1981. 36(3): 13-15.

Chesness, Robert A. "Fifty Years of Deer Hunting." *The Minnesota Volunteer.* November/December, 1979. 42(247): 58-62.

Cook, Sam. "Backtracking." *Petersen's Hunting.* October 1980. p. 105.

_____. "More Than the Hunt." *Wisconsin State Journal.* Dec. 2, 1990.

Craft, Karen Peterson & Dr. Robert Jackson. "Is There a Woman in Your Hunting Party?" *Iowa Conservationist.* January, 1989. 48(1): 12-13.

Dale, Bob. "Old Camp in the Swamp." *Mississippi Game and Fish.* November/December, 1972. 35(6): 18.

"Deer Camp Poker Games." *Wisconsin Sportsman.* November/December, 1963. pp. 37-39.

Dickey, Charley. "Deer Camps: Neat, Clean and Otherwise." *North American Whitetail.* July/August, 1983. 2(3): 34, 74-75.

Dietz, Lew. "Deer Camp on Wheels." *Field & Stream.* December, 1963. pp. 37-39.

_____. "Whitetail Challenge." *Outdoor Life.* October, 1978. p. 70.

Durfresne, Frank. "California Deer Camp." *Field & Stream.* August, 1964. pp. 36-37.

Erickson, Cal. "Miracle Cherub Lodge." *Wisconsin Natural Resources.* November/December, 1980. 4(6): 6-8.

Evans, Carol. "Use of Hunting Clubs as Management Units." *Human Dimensions in Wildlife Newsletter.* Summer, 1990. 9(3): 24-25.

Fegely, Tom. "Deer Camp." *Buckmasters Whitetail Magazine.* December, 1988. 2(5): 78-79.

Fleming, Kay M. "Quality White-Tailed Deer Management on an East Texas Hunting Club." 1983 Proceedings of the Annual Conference of the Southeastern Association of Fish & Wildlife Agencies. pp. 118-126.

Frimodig, Mac. "The Mosquito Lake Culture Club." *Michigan Natural Resources.* November/December, 1972. pp. 18-22.

Glading, Ben. "The Role of Private Hunting Clubs in California." 1969 Proceedings of the Western Association of Fish & Wildlife Agencies. Volume 48. pp. 129-141.

Greer, Dave. "Deer Camp: What it's all About." *Whitetails.* Winter 1991. pp. 33-34.

Grenko, Ronald. "Coal Camp Nimrods." *New Mexico Wildlife.* November/December, 1988. 33(6): 22-25.

Guynn, David C. Jr., et. al. "Cooperative Management of White-Tailed Deer on Private Lands in Mississippi." *Wildlife Society Bulletin.* 1983. 11(3): 211-214.

Harper, William D. "Articles of Partnership for the Deer Shack." *Deer & Deer Hunting.* May/June, 1981. 4(5): 29-32.

Hazelworth, Maureen S. & Beth E. Wilson. "The Effects of an Outdoor Adventure Camp Experience on Self-Concept." *The Journal of*

Environmental Education. Summer, 1990. 21(4): 33-37.

Hinkelman, Jon. "The Camp." *Deer & Deer Hunting.* November, 1989. 13(3): 10-11.

Holm, Randy "Hawkeye." "The Wild Bunch Camp." *Deer & Deer Hunting.* November/December, 1977. 1(1): 5-6.

Hunt Club Digest: The Official Publication of the Forest Landowners Association. Alabama: Vulcan Outdoors. August, 2000.

"Hunt Club Management: Work or Play?" *On Target.* Fall, 1990. 5(1): 1.

Hunter, Gerald R. "Outrageous Deer Camp Shenanigans." *Georgia Sportsman.* December, 1980. pp. 36-37.

"Hunting Club Liability is Serious Business." *Willamette Wildlife.* Fall, 1990. 4(3): 3.

Jackson, Bud. "The Role of Sportsmen's Clubs in Conservation." *Louisana Conservationist.* February, 1954. 6(5): 6-8.

Jackson, Lawrence W. "The Role of Camps in Relation to Deer Hunting in the Town of Malone." *New York Fish and Game Journal.* January, 1975. 22(1): 13-24.

Jackson, Robert. "Who Are We?" *Archery World.* 1984. 33(2): 16, 48-50.

_____. "Compound Intensity: The Wisconsin Bowhunter." *Wisconsin Natural Resources.* November/December, 1983. pp. 12-16.

_____, & Robert Norton. "The Last Hunt." *Wisconsin Natural Resources.* November/December, 1980. 4(6): 5-12.

_____. "Deer Hunting is a Family Affair." *Wisconsin Natural Resources.* November/December, 1979. pp. 10-15.

Jones, Robert F. "Brothers of the Wolf: Deer Camp Through the Ages." *Sports Afield.* November, 2000. pp. 66-69.

Jurek, Judy Bishop. "Around the Campfire." *Texas Parks & Wildlife.* October, 1992. 50(10): 14-15.

Kelly, George H. "The Sagamore Fish and Game Club." *Forest and Stream.* April 1, 1899. p. 245.

Kennedy, James J. "Motivation and Rewards of Hunting in a Group Versus Along." *Wildlife Society Bulletin.* Spring, 1974. 29(1): 3-7.

Kennedy, Russ. "Deer CAMP (What If ????)." *Kentucky Happy Hunting Ground.* September/October, 1990. 46(5): 10-12.

Kinton, Tony. "Duffin Hunting Club." *Mississippi Outdoors.* November/December, 1999. 62(6): 24-26.

Klessig, Lowell L. "Hunting: Savage Instinct or Communion with Nature?" *Wisconsin Academy Review.* 1973. 20(1): 12-14.

Kulpa, Jack. "Deercampsia Hypomnesia." *Field & Stream.* October,

1985. pp. 46-48.

LaFreniere, L. A. "Dos and Don'ts of Deer Camp." *North American Whitetail.* October, 1993. 12(6): 17-19.

Langford, Carl. "Looking Back Over Forty Years at Steele Bayou Hunting Club." *The Habitat.* November, 1988. 5(2):3.

Lee, Robert G. "Alone with Others: The Paradox of Privacy in Wilderness." *Leisure Sciences.* 1977. (1): 3-19.

"Magnolia — More Than Just a Hunting club." *The Habitat.* November, 1985. 2(2): 1, 8.

Mason, Dorothy S. "Private Deer Hunting on the Coastal Plain of North Carolina." *Southeastern Geographer.* May, 1989. 29(1): 1-16.

Matthews, Renny. "Deer Camp Not All Fun." *Mississippi Game & Fish.* 1974. 37(6): 12.

"Mississippi Deer Camp Scene in 1897." *Mississippi Game and Fish.* December, 1950. 14(6): 7.

Moen, Aaron N. "The Modern Deer CAMP." *Deer & Deer Hunting.* March/April, 1986. 9(4): 8-15.

Morris, Deborah. "Guess Who's Coming to Deer Camp?" *Outdoor Life.* December, 1990. pp. 55-56.

Morrissey, William J. "The Diana Hunting Club." *Wisconsin Sportsman.* November/December, 1982. 11(6): 24-27.

Nelson, Bill. "Five Decades of Hunting Spoofs." *The Milwaukee Journal Magazine.* Nov. 11, 1990. pp. 6-13.

Ozoga, John J. "Camp Comfort." *Deer & Deer Hunting.* November, 1998. 22(4): 64-71.

Pass, Aaron. "The Deer Camp, the Company, the Hunt." *Georgia Sportsman.* September, 1981. pp. 19-22.

Randolph, John. "The Stumpsitters." *Outdoor Life.* February, 1979. Volume 163. pp. 60-63.

_____. "Deer Camp." *Outdoor Life.* October, 1979. pp. 84-89.

Richey, David. "Deer Camp: The Place I Want to Be." *Sportsman's Hunting,* 1982. pp. 38-41.

_____. "Joys of a Deer Camp." *Sports Afield Deer Annual,* 1990. pp. 76-82.

_____. "Deer Camps of Yesteryear." *North American Whitetail.* Premier Issue, 1983. 1(1): 50-55.

Robinson, Jerome B. "Deer Camp." *Sports Afield.* October 1983. pp. 76-78.

Roden, Bill. "New York's Whitetail Hunting Legacy: The Adirondacks." *North American Whitetail.* February, 1984. 3(2): 6, 62-66.

Robert C. Ruark. "Dixie Deer Hunt." *Saturday Evening Post.* Oct. 26, 1946. pp. 25+.

Saile, Bob. "The Deer Hunting Camp." *Field & Stream.* May, 1986. Volume 91. pp. 101+

Sasser, Ray. "What a Deer Camp Ought to Be." *Sports Afield Deer Annual.* 1982. p. 96.

Scherl, Lea M. "Self in Wilderness: Understanding the Psychological Benefits of Individual-Wilderness Interaction Through Self-Control." *Leisure Sciences.* 1989. 11(2): 123-135.

Schneider, Gary. "Our Bunch." *Wisconsin Hunting and Fishing News.* 1977. pp. 8-9.

Schwalbach, Randall P. "Return to Deer Camp." *Deer & Deer Hunting.* March, 1990. 13(5): 90-92.

Scott, Neil R. "Toward a Psychology of Wilderness Experience." *Natural Resources Journal.* April, 1974. p. 231-237.

Sipos, Carol L. "Just Us Girls." *Pennsylvania Game News.* April, 1989. 60(4): 25-29.

Sleigh, Samuel J. "Remembering the First Fifty Years." *Pennsylvania Game News.* June, 1988. 59(6): 24-30.

Slovensky, Charles. "How to Run a Deer Camp." *Deer & Deer Hunting.* November/December, 1980. 4(2): 29-31.

Smith, Edmund Ware. "Jake's Rangers Hunt the Whitetail." *Deer & Deer Hunting.* August, 1983. 6(6): 34-44.

Smith, Richard P. "Women's Deer Camp Opens." *Deer & Deer Hunting.* November, 1991. 15(4): 85-86.

Sodders, Betty. "Blaney Rod & Gun Club's Historic Past." *Whitetails Unlimited.* Spring/Summer, 1999. pp. 18—20, 45.

Stelter, Vern. "Cuisine Du Hunting Camp." *Wyoming Wildlife.* September 1988. 52(9): 4-5.

"Successful Deer Management in East Texas North Boggy & Coon Pond Hunting Club." *Wildlife Resources.* March, 1991. 1(1): 1-2.

Taylor, Buck. "Deer Camp Essentials." *Baker Deer Hunting.* 1987. pp. 47-50.

"The Deer Hunters." *Wisconsin State Journal.* Nov. 29, 1991. p. 1c.

"The Good Life to be Found in a Wisconsin Deer Camp." *Wisconsin Sportsman.* November/December, 1975. 4(6): 8-9.

"The Hunter's Camp." *Forest and Stream.* June 29, 1876. 6(21): 1.

Towsley, Bryce. "Deer Camp." *Buckmasters Whitetail Magazine.* November, 2000. 14(4): 80-88.

Trueblood, Ted. "The Hunter's Camp." *Field & Stream.* October 1980. pp. 34-36.

Twight, Ben W., et. al. "Privacy and Camping: Closeness to the Self vs. Closeness to Others." *Leisure Sciences.* 1981. 4(4): 427-441.

Van Der Puy, Nick. "Deer Camp: Roughing it in Style!" *Wisconsin Sportsman.* September/October, 1981. pp. 54-57.

Vance, Joel M. "The Decline and Fall of the Hunting Shack." *Gray's Sporting Journal.* Fall, 1976. 1(5): 10-14.

Vincent, Jim. "The Great Escape." *The Complete Deer Hunting Annual.* 1990. pp. 42-43.

"Wagon Wheel Hunting Club." *Willamette Wildlife.* Winter, 1988. 2(1): 6.

Wegner, Robert. "The Stump Sitters: Leopold's Prophesy Fulfilled?" *Cynegeticus: A Publication Devoted to the Interdisciplinary Study of Hunting.* October, 1979. 3(4): 2-7.

_____. "Deer Camp". *Deer & Deer Hunting.* November/December, 1980. 4(2): 12-19.

_____. "The Deer Club: The Wave of the Future." *Deer & Deer Hunting.* October, 1991. 15(3): 18-30.

Wootters, John. "A Field Guide to Odd Birds Seen in Hunting Camp." *Petersen's Hunting.* January, 1989. pp. 70-72.

Young, Robert A., & Rick Crandall. "Wilderness Use and Self-Actualization." *Journal of Leisure Research.* Second Quarter. 1984. pp. 149-160.

Zumbo, Jim. "The Horn Hunters." *Outdoor Life.* December, 1983. Volume 172. pp. 46-47.

Theses, Abstracts, Pamphlets, Etc.

Bartlett, I. H. "Lost Lake Woods Club." Michigan Department of Conservation Report #2022. October 8, 1954.

Collier, Bret & Lynette Duncan. "Use of Cluster-Sampling Metholdogy to Survey Deer Hunt Club Members in Arkansas." Abstract of the 24th Southeast Deer Study Group Meeting, 2001.

Cringan, A. T. "Report on 1951 Non-Resident Deer Hunting from Licenced Camps in the Sioux Lookout District." Ontario Department of Lands and Forest. *Wildlife Management Bulletin* #3. 1952.

Daggett, David. "Sawyer Swampers: The First Fifteen Years." Wisconsin: Privately printed, 1979.

Duncan, R. W., & V. P. Kopf. "Response by Landowners and Hunt Clubs to Two New Deer Management Programs in Virginia." Abstract of the 12th Southeast Deer Study Group Meeting, 1989. p. 6.

Evans, Carol K. "Use of Hunting Clubs as Management Units."

Masters Thesis. Stephen F. Austin State University, 1989.

_____, & James C. Kroll. "Hunting Clubs: Who are They and What are They Doing?" Abstract of the 12th Southeast Deer Study Group Meeting, 1989. p. 7.

Gibson, Herman, III. "Deer Hunting Clubs in Concordia Parish: The Role of Male Sodalities in the Maintenance of Social Values." Master's Thesis. Louisiana State University, 1976.

Gottschalk, Gordon. "History of Buckshot, Incoporated, 1956-1986." Wisconsin: Privately printed, 1987.

Hackett, Edward J., et. al. "The Deer Club Association: An Efficient and Manageable Unit." Abstract of the 4th Southeast Deer Study Group Meeting, 1981. pp. 4-5.

Harlow, Richard F., & David C. Guynn Jr. "Land Owners and Hunting Clubs." *Southeastern Deer Study Group Annotated Bibliography, 1977-1990.* pp. 169-173.

Hill, Thomas A. "Measurements of Attitude Change in Members of a Hunting Club." Master's Thesis. Mississippi State University, 1980.

Hofacker, Al. "The Stump Sitters' Story." Wisconsin: Unpublished Manuscript, n. d. 11 pp.

"Hunting Club Officers' Manual." International Paper, 1987.

Jackson, Lawrence W. "A Survey of Camps in Malone Town." Pittman Robertson Project W-89-R-17: XI-5, Janauary 24, 1973.

Johnson, Steven C. "Implications of Deer Club Leasing on Deer Herd Management in Georgia." Abstract of the 14th Southeast Deer Study Group Meeting, 1991. p. 20.

Klessig, Lowell L. "Hunting: Social Beginnings and Social Endings." Paper presented at a Conference on Hunting: Sport or Sin? Wisconsin: Stevens Point. Sept. 14, 1974.

Lefes, William S. "The Sociology of Deer Hunting in Two Pennsylvania Counties, 1951." Master's Thesis. Pennsylvania State College, 1953.

Manierre, "Franny." "The Story of the Clow Deer Hunt." Michigan: Privately printed pamphlet, 1938.

Mckelvy, Charles L., & Mark C. Conner. "Implications of Quality Deer Management on a Northeast Florida Hunting Club." Abstract of the 11th Southeast Deer Study Group Meeting, 1988. p. 9.

McMath, Neil. "Continuing the Story of Turtle Lake." Michigan: Mimeographed Document, n.d.

McQueen, John D. "A Factual History of 'Dollarhide.'" Alabama: Privately printed pamphlet, 1943.

Millen, George W. "Blizzard Bound — 1914: An Account of Deer Hunting at Camp Newton." Michigan: Privately printed pamphlet, 1914.

Moreland, David M. "Do Hunting Clubs Want Deer Management?" Abstract of the 10th Southeast Deer Study Group, 1987. p. 10.

_____, & Leslie Johnson. "Quality Deer Management Without Mandatory Regulations." Abstract of the 18th Southeast Deer Study Group Meeting, 1995. pp. 29-30.

New, Harry S. "The Story of the Turtle Lake Deer Club." Michigan: Mimeographed Document, 1923.

Rehfield, Chet. "Chronicle of a Deer Hunt at Riley Creek Meadows in the Malheur National Forest in Oregon." Oregon: Privately printed, 1939.

Simonson, Vern. "The Cayuga Deer Slayers, 1966." Wisconsin: Edited and printed by Thomas A. Heberlein, 1983.

Staten, Charles M. "Effects of a Deer Management Assistance Program on Nine Hunting Clubs in the Mississippi Delta." Abstract of the 14th Southeast Deer Study Group Meeting, 1991. pp. 19-20.

Still, H. R. Jr., et. al. "Quality Deer Management on Industrial Forests." Abstract of the 10th Southeast Deer Study Group, 1987. p. 11.

Tappe, Philip A. & Richard A. Williams. "Differences Between Arkansas Hunt Clubs in Quality Deer Management and Traditional Deer Management Programs." Abstract of the 19th Southeast Deer Study Group Meeting, 1996. p. 6.

_____. "Characteristics, Attitudes and Perceptions of Arkansas Hunt Clubs in Quality Deer Management and Traditional Deer Management Programs." Abstract of the 18th Southeast Deer Study Group Meeting, 1995. p. 22.

Thackston, R.E., & T.L. Ivey. "Characteristics of Clubs Requesting Technical Assistance for Deer Management." Abstract of the 12th Southeast Deer Study Group Meeting, 1989. pp. 6-7.

"'The Mahannah Association:' A Case Study in Deer Management." Abstract of the 10th Southeast Deer Study Group, 1987. p. 11.

Wileden. A. F. "The Buckshot Story, 1928-1972." Wisconsin: Privately printed pamphlet, n. d.

_____. "A Lifetime of Hunting and Fishing Experiences." Wisconsin: Privately printed, 1982.

Wilson, Rev. Robert. "An Address Delivered Before the St. John's Hunting Club." South Carolina: Privately printed, 1907.

Woods, Grant R., et. al. "Hunting Clubs' Perception of Quality Deer Management in Mississippi and South Carolina." Abstract of the 16th Southeast Deer Study Group Meeting, 1993. pp. 13-14.

ABOUT THE AUTHOR

In 1979, Robert Wegner received his Ph.D. from the University of Wisconsin-Madison where he was trained as a cultural historian. After a short-term teaching career at the university, he became the editor and, later, a co-owner of *Deer & Deer Hunting* magazine. After the magazine was sold to Krause Publications in 1992, he became a free-lance writer specializing in the cultural history of white-tailed deer and deer hunting.

His work has appeared in such magazines as *Deer & Deer Hunting, Quality Whitetails, North American Hunter, Wisconsin Trails, Whitetail Hunting Strategies, Wisconsin Outdoor Journal* and many others. His landmark book trilogy, *Deer &*

Deer Hunting, has sold more than 100,000 copies. Fred Bear referred to this three-volume work as "a classic in American hunting literature."

Wegner resides in Deer Valley, a secluded land filled with whitetails and wild turkeys in the heart of "the Uplands," in southwestern Wisconsin with his wife, Maren, and daughter, Serena. Wegner has studied, observed and hunted whitetails more than 40 years.

If you want to share your deer camp stories and photos for future publications, Wegner can be reached at: Deer Valley, 6008 K, Blue Mounds, WI 53517. Or call (608-) 795-2721. For fax, (608) 795-4720. For e-mail, robert_wegner@angelfire.com.

ACKNOWLEDGMENTS

The author is greatly indebted to the following individuals, institutions, historical museums and private art collections: Jennifer Pillath, Patrick Durkin, Debbie Knauer, Carol Lueder/Fair Chase Inc., Kenyon C. Bolton III, State Historical Society of Wisconsin, The Detroit Institute of Art, Western Reserve Historical Society, Shelburne Museum in Shelburne, Vt., Adirondack Museum in Blue Mountain Lake, N.Y., Stark Museum of Art in Orange, Texas, Michigan Historical Collection/Bentley Historical Library/University of Michigan, Thomas A. Heberlein, Ph.D., Valerius Geist, Ph.D., The Marquette County Historical Society in Marquette, Mich., National Geographic Society, Philadelphia Museum of Art, Larry Huffman/Legendary Whitetails Collection, C.M. Russell Museum in Great Falls, Mont., Theodore Roosevelt Collection, Harvard College Library, Amon Carter Museum in Fort Worth, Texas, Jack Brittingham, Marshall Huffman, Chip Cooper, Fred P. "Wigs" Lund, Mert Cowley, Michigan Historical Society, Cornell University/HDRU, Minnesota Historical Society, National Wildlife Federation, University of Wisconsin-Madison/Archives, Sid Richardson Collection of Western Art in Fort Worth, Texas, A.F. Wileden Collection, Roger Wollin Collection, Ned Smith, Larry Zach, Mississippi Department of Archives and History, John Madson, Michigan Department of State/State Archives, Florence Huffman Collection, David Kowalski.

ALSO BY THE AUTHOR

Deer & Deer Hunting, Book 1
Deer & Deer Hunting, Book 2
Deer & Deer Hunting, Book 3
Wegner's Bibliography on Deer & Deer Hunting